Preface

In an era where data is often hailed as the new oil, the significance of effectively storing, managing, and analyzing this data has never been more crucial. Organizations across the globe are increasingly relying on data to drive their decision-making processes, enhance customer experiences, and stay ahead of the competition. This reliance underscores the importance of the fields of Data Warehousing and Data Mining, which are central to transforming raw data into actionable insights.

This book is crafted to provide a comprehensive introduction to the intertwined worlds of Data Warehousing and Data Mining. Whether you are a student, a data professional, or someone with a curiosity about how data can be leveraged to uncover hidden patterns and drive business success, this book is designed to meet your needs.

Data Warehousing serves as the bedrock for storing vast amounts of data in a manner that is both organized and accessible. It involves the creation of a centralized repository where data from various sources is integrated, cleansed, and made ready for analysis. The structured environment of a data warehouse ensures that data is reliable and consistent, which is essential for making informed decisions.

Data Mining, on the other hand, is the process of exploring and analyzing large datasets to discover meaningful patterns, trends, and relationships. Through the use of sophisticated algorithms and techniques, data mining enables organizations to predict future trends, identify new opportunities, and gain deeper insights into their operations.

This book is structured to guide you through the essential concepts and techniques of Data Warehousing and Data Mining. It begins with foundational topics and progressively delves into more complex areas, ensuring that readers develop a robust understanding of the subject matter. Practical examples and case studies are provided to illustrate how these concepts are applied in real-world scenarios, helping to bridge the gap between theory and practice.

Our goal with this book is to equip you with the knowledge and skills necessary to harness the power of data within your organization. Whether you are embarking on a new project or looking to enhance existing systems, this book will serve as a valuable resource on your journey.

Table of Contents

Master Of Computer Applications (MCA)
Chapter 1: Term-End Examinations, December, 2021
MCS-221: Data Warehousing and Data Mining

Time: 3 Hours
Maximum Marks: 100
Weightage: 70

Note: Question No. 1 is compulsory. Answer any three Questions from the rest.

1. (a) Define a Data Warehouse. List and explain the four characteristics of a Data Warehouse. 10

(b) Explain the following OLAP architectures and draw their architectural diagram : 10
(i) Multidimensional Online Analytical Processing (MOLAP)
(ii) Hybrid Online Analytical Processing (HOLAP)

(c) Define "data cleaning" which is a data preprocessing technique. In this context, explain the concept of Noisy data cleaning along with some suitable examples. 10

(d) What is a Decision Tree ? How is it useful in classification ? With the help of an example, explain the process of construction of a decision tree and its representation. 10

2. (a) What is Text Mining ? Where is it used ? Explain any two text mining techniques with the help of a suitable example for each. 10

(b) In the context of mining multimedia data on the web, explain the following terms : 10
(i) Page Rank
(ii) Hits
(iii) Page Layout Analysis
(iv) Vision Page Segmentation

3. (a) Define a Data Lake. Explain the step-by-step process of creating a data lake. 10

(b) With the help of an example, explain the star schema dimensional model. 10

4. (a) What is Metadata ? What are its contents ? Justify how metadata can be an important component in Data Warehousing ? Also mention its types. 10

(b) Explain the three components of ETL. Also mention how to improve the ETL performance. 10

5. Write short notes on any four of the following : 4*5=20
(a) Data Marts
(b) Association Rule Generation
(c) Apriori Algorithm
(d) Clustering and its Methods
(e) Bayes' Theorem

Master Of Computer Applications (MCA)
Chapter 2: Term-End Examination, June, 2022
MCS-221: Data Warehousing and Data Mining

Time: 3 Hours
Maximum Marks: 100
Weightage: 70

Note: (i) Question No. 1 is compulsory.
(ii) Answer any three Questions from the rest.

1. (a) What is Association Rule Mining ? With reference to this, explain the concepts given below : 10
(i) Support Count
(ii) Frequent Item set
(iii) Association Rule
(iv) Rule Evaluation metrics

(b) Define classification. With the help of an example for each, explain the following classification models : 10

(i) Descriptive modeling
(ii) Predictive modeling

(c) Describe the snowflake schema multidimensional modeling technique. Give an example and illustrate it. List its pros and cons. 10

(d) What is complex data modeling ? Where is this used ? Explain "Anchor" complex data model. 10

2. (a) List and describe all the four types of OLAP operations. 10

(b) Define text mining. Mention any three applications of it. What are the various techniques used to analyze the web-usage patterns ? 10

3. (a) Define a data warehouse. List and explain all the 3 types of data warehouses. 10

(b) What is data transformation ? List and explain all the data transformation steps. 10

4. (a) What is data mining ? List out the key differences between data warehousing and data mining. Mention any four applications of data mining. 10

(b) What is ETL ? Why do you need ETL in data warehouses ? Also, explain how ETL works in Data Warehousing ? 10

5. Write short notes on any four of the following : 4*5=20
(a) OLTP
(b) Data Marts
(c) Web structure mining
(d) Cloud Data Warehousing
(e) Data Granularity

Master Of Computer Applications (MCA)
Chapter 3: Term-End Examination, December, 2022
MCS-221: Data Warehousing and Data Mining

Time: 3 Hours
Maximum Marks: 100
Weightage: 70

Note: Question No. 1 is compulsory. Answer any three Questions from the rest.

1. (a) Define Dimensional Modelling. With reference to this, define the terms Facts, Fact Table, Dimensions and Dimensional Table. Give an example use-case and derive fact table and dimension tables. 10

(b) With the help of a Data Warehouse Architecture diagram, explain the following components and their significance: 10

(i) ETL
(ii) Metadata
(iii) Data Warehouse Access Tools
(iv) Data Warehouse Reporting Layer

(c) Define a Decision Tree. With the help of an example, explain the construction and representation of decision tree. Also, mention its strengths and weaknesses. 10

(d) Discuss the following categories of Data Mining Issues : 10
(i) Mining Methodology and User Iteration Issues
(ii) Performance-based Issues
(iii) Diverse Data Types Issues

2. (a) Define Data Cleaning. Explain the ways and means of handling the Missing Values and Noisy Data while data preprocessing. 10

(b) Write and explain the K-means algorithm for clustering. How does it work ? 10

3. (a) Why does dimensionality reduction of text need to be done ? Explain Tokenization process and Vector from text approach, with the help of a suitable example for each. 10

(b) Enumerate the best practices for Data Warehouse Architecture. 5

(c) Describe the following types of data marts : 5
(i) Dependent data marts
(ii) Independent data marts

4. (a) With the help of an example use-case, explain the Snowflake schema. List its advantages and disadvantages. 10

(b) Define Web Mining. What kind of tasks can be performed using it ? Discuss its features and also a few applications. 10

5. Write short notes on the following : 4*5=20
(a) Data Transformation (with reference to data preprocessing)
(b) Cloud Data Warehousing
(c) Data Lake and its Architecture
(d) Data Warehouse Automation

Master Of Computer Applications (MCA)
Chapter 4: Term-End Examination, June, 2023
MCS-227: Data Warehousing and Data Mining

Time: 3 Hours
Maximum Marks: 100
Weightage: 70

Note: (i) Question No. 1 is compulsory.
(ii) Answer any three Questions from the rest.

1. (a) Discuss the following data preprocessing stages briefly : 10
(i) Data Cleaning
(ii) Data Integration
(iii) Data Reduction
(iv) Data Transformation

(b) Define Aggregate fact tables and derived dimension tables. What are their significance ? Give an example. Also mention their advantages and disadvantages. 10

(c) Enumerate the key challenges in data warehouse design. 5

(d) Differentiate between a data lake and a data warehouse. 5

(e) Write and explain the Apriori algorithm to identify the most frequently occurring elements and meaningful associations in a dataset. 10

2. (a) What is Cluster Analysis ? How is this used in Data Mining ? Give an example. Also mention few applications of cluster analysis in data mining. 10

(b) List and discuss various types of Web-mining. 10

3. (a) Explain the following techniques for Dimensionality Reduction : 10
(i) Feature Selection
(ii) Feature Extraction

(b) Discuss the layered implementation of ETL in a Data Warehouse. 10

4. (a) Define OLAP. Differentiate between Multicube and Hypercube. Mention the applications of OLAP reporting system. 10
(b) List and explain the following types of Data Warehouses : 10
(i) Enterprise Data Warehouse (EDW)
(ii) Operational Data Store

5. Write short notes on the following : 4*s5=20
(a) ELT vs. ETL
(b) Data Marts
(c) Applictions of Data Mining
(d) OLAP data cube operations

Master Of Computer Applications (MCA)
Chapter 5: Term-End Examination, December, 2023
MCS-227: Data Warehousing and Data Mining

Time: 3 Hours
Maximum Marks: 100
Weightage: 70

Note: (i) Question No. 1 is compulsory.
(ii) Answer any three Questions from the rest.

1. (a) With the help of a diagram, describe the Conceptual Architecture of Hadoop Data Warehouse. 10
(b) Draw and explain star schema diagram and snow-flake schema diagram for the dimensions (Products, Customers, Time, Locations) and fact (Sales-Items) for the measures namely Quantity-sold and Amount-sold for a manufacturing company data warehouse dimensional modeling. 10
(b) What is load-balancing ? Why is it imperative in cloud computing to balance the cloud-load ? Also, explain briefly hardware-based load balancer and virtual load balancer. 10
(c) Define Noisy data while doing data pre-processing. Delete the noise with Binning smoothing techniques for the following details using partition in Bins (Equal-frequency) :

4, 2, 6, 10, 8, 16, 12, 24, 22, 14, 26

stored price details (in dollars). 10
(d) Define Clustering in Data Mining. Write and explain k-means clustering algorithm. List its advantages and disadvantages. 10

2. (a) What is Web-Mining ? List various web-mining tasks. Also, discuss the following types of web-mining: 10
(i) Web content mining
(ii) Web usage mining

(b) With the help of an example, explain rule-based classification. 5
(c) What are the various steps involved in building a classification model ? Explain with the help of an example. 5

3. (a) With the help of an example, explain Market Basket Analysis. 5
(b) Write and explain Apriori algorithm used to identify the most frequently occurring elements and meaningful associations in any dataset. 10
(c) List and discuss any two popular data mining tools. 5

4. (a) Discuss ETL and its need. Explain in detail, all the steps involved in ETL with the help of a suitable diagram. 10
(b) List and explain any three key challenges of Data Warehouse. 3
(c) With reference to Alex Gorelik, explain the following additional data lake stages : 7
(i) Data Puddle
(ii) Data Pond
(iii) Data Lake
(iv) Data Ocean

5. Write short notes on the following : 4*5=20
(a) Aggregate fact table and derived dimensional tables
(b) Data swamp
(c) Data Preprocessing stages
(d) Agglomerative approach of Hierarchical method

Chapter 6: Most Asked Questions Part-A

1. What is data warehousing, and why is it important in modern businesses?
Answer: Data warehousing is a technology used to collect, store, and manage large volumes of data from different sources in a centralized repository, optimized for query and analysis rather than transaction processing. It allows organizations to consolidate data from multiple systems, enabling more efficient reporting, business intelligence, and decision-making processes. By using data warehouses, businesses gain insights through historical data analysis, trend forecasting, and pattern recognition. The structured nature of a data warehouse supports data consistency, data quality, and provides a strong foundation for data mining, making it essential for strategic planning in today's competitive landscape.

2. What are the main characteristics of a data warehouse?
Answer: The main characteristics of a data warehouse are subject-oriented, integrated, non-volatile, and time-variant. Subject-oriented means the warehouse is organized around key subjects like sales, inventory, or finance rather than specific applications. Integrated signifies that data is collected from various sources and standardized. Non-volatile implies that data is stable and does not change frequently once entered into the warehouse. Time-variant indicates that historical data is maintained for trend analysis and forecasting. These characteristics ensure that a data warehouse is optimized for analytical tasks, offering consistent, reliable data for decision-making and reporting.

3. How does a data warehouse differ from a database?
Answer: A data warehouse differs from a traditional database in its purpose, structure, and usage. Databases are designed for real-time transaction processing (OLTP), focusing on data input, updates, and quick responses to routine queries. In contrast, data warehouses are built for online analytical processing (OLAP), which emphasizes large-scale analysis, complex queries, and historical data trends. While databases handle current data and support daily operations, warehouses store vast amounts of historical data, enabling strategic business insights. Additionally, data warehouses are optimized for read-heavy operations, whereas databases handle frequent read/write tasks.

4. What is the ETL process in data warehousing?
Answer: ETL stands for Extract, Transform, and Load. It is a critical process in data warehousing that ensures data is collected from diverse sources, cleaned, transformed, and loaded into the data warehouse. Extraction involves retrieving data from different source systems. Transformation involves cleansing, formatting, and applying business rules to ensure consistency and quality. Loading refers to inserting the transformed data into the data warehouse for analysis. ETL processes are vital for ensuring data integrity, standardization, and usability. Efficient ETL operations enable accurate reporting and support decision-making in data-driven organizations.

5. What is OLAP and how is it used in data warehousing?
Answer: OLAP, or Online Analytical Processing, is a technology used to perform multidimensional analysis of data stored in a data warehouse. It allows users to quickly retrieve and analyze data across various dimensions like time, geography, or product. OLAP systems support complex analytical queries such as roll-up, drill-down, slice, and dice, enabling interactive data exploration. There are different OLAP types—MOLAP, ROLAP, and HOLAP—each with unique storage and processing methods. OLAP is widely used in business intelligence for trend analysis, forecasting, and strategic planning due to its fast performance and intuitive multidimensional data representation.

6. What are fact tables and dimension tables in a data warehouse?
Answer: Fact tables and dimension tables are the core components of a data warehouse schema. Fact tables store quantitative data—metrics or measurements—such as sales amount, revenue, or profit, and they usually have foreign keys that reference dimension tables. Dimension tables contain descriptive attributes related to the facts, such as customer details, product information, or time periods. This structure enables efficient querying and analysis. For example, a sales fact table may include dimensions like customer, product, and time. Proper design of fact and dimension tables is essential for effective data modeling and OLAP analysis.

7. What is a star schema in data warehouse design?
Answer: A star schema is a simple and commonly used data warehouse schema where a central fact table is connected to multiple dimension tables, resembling a star shape. The fact table holds numerical metrics, and each dimension table contains descriptive data that provides context to those facts. Star schemas simplify query performance, improve

data retrieval speed, and are easy to understand. They support efficient slicing and dicing in OLAP operations. This schema is ideal for straightforward analytical needs where data redundancy is acceptable in favor of performance and simplicity.

8. What is a snowflake schema, and how does it differ from a star schema?
Answer: A snowflake schema is a normalized form of a star schema in which dimension tables are further broken down into related sub-dimension tables, resulting in a complex, multi-level structure. While the star schema has a simple, denormalized design that improves query speed, the snowflake schema reduces data redundancy through normalization, leading to a more complex database structure. Snowflake schemas are suitable for environments where data integrity and space optimization are prioritized. However, they can lead to slower query performance compared to star schemas due to the increased number of joins.

9. What is data mining, and how does it relate to data warehousing?
Answer: Data mining is the process of discovering patterns, correlations, trends, and useful information from large datasets using statistical, machine learning, and artificial intelligence techniques. It is often performed on data stored in a data warehouse, which provides a clean, consolidated source of historical and transactional data. While a data warehouse enables storage and retrieval of data, data mining extracts actionable insights and knowledge from that data. Common data mining tasks include classification, clustering, regression, and association rule mining, which are critical for predictive analytics, fraud detection, and customer behavior analysis.

10. What are the main applications of data mining in real-world scenarios?
Answer: Data mining has numerous real-world applications across various industries. In retail, it is used for market basket analysis, customer segmentation, and sales forecasting. In finance, data mining supports fraud detection, risk management, and credit scoring. Healthcare uses data mining for disease prediction, patient segmentation, and treatment effectiveness analysis. In marketing, it helps optimize campaigns, target customers, and analyze sentiment. Manufacturing benefits from predictive maintenance and quality control, while telecommunications use it for churn analysis. Overall, data mining transforms raw data into strategic intelligence, enhancing operational efficiency and competitive advantage.

11. What is the role of metadata in a data warehouse?
Answer: Metadata in a data warehouse serves as the "data about data," providing information about the structure, operations, and usage of the data stored. It includes descriptions of data sources, data types, transformation rules, data lineage, and user access rights. Metadata helps users and tools understand where data comes from, how it's been processed, and how it can be used. It improves data governance, simplifies data discovery, and ensures consistency across data environments. Effective metadata management enhances data quality, enables better ETL process control, and supports business users in making informed decisions.

12. What is data cube in OLAP?
Answer: A data cube in OLAP represents multidimensional data, allowing users to analyze data across multiple dimensions simultaneously. Each cell in the cube contains aggregated data, such as sales amount, calculated based on dimensions like product, geography, and time. Data cubes facilitate fast retrieval and complex querying operations like roll-up, drill-down, slice, and dice. They offer an intuitive way to perform analysis by organizing data in a 3D matrix format, helping decision-makers identify trends, patterns, and relationships in large datasets with speed and efficiency.

13. What are surrogate keys in data warehousing?
Answer: Surrogate keys are system-generated unique identifiers used in data warehouse dimension tables to uniquely identify a record. Unlike natural or business keys (like customer IDs), surrogate keys have no business meaning and are often sequential integers. They simplify data integration, ensure uniqueness, and help maintain consistency when the same entity appears with different natural keys across various source systems. Surrogate keys are especially useful in slowly changing dimensions, where historical data must be tracked without altering existing relationships in the fact table.

14. What are slowly changing dimensions (SCD) in data warehousing?
Answer: Slowly Changing Dimensions (SCDs) refer to dimension attributes that change over time but not frequently, such as a customer's address or job title. Managing these changes is crucial to maintaining historical accuracy. There

are several types of SCDs: Type 1 overwrites old data; Type 2 creates new records to preserve history; Type 3 adds new columns to track changes. Proper handling of SCDs ensures that historical data in fact tables remains consistent and that analytical results reflect accurate timelines and contexts.

15. What is data mart and how does it differ from a data warehouse?
Answer: A data mart is a subset of a data warehouse focused on a specific business line or department, such as sales, marketing, or finance. While a data warehouse is enterprise-wide and contains integrated data from all departments, a data mart is tailored for localized decision-making. Data marts are smaller, easier to implement, and offer faster query performance for departmental needs. They can be dependent (sourced from the central data warehouse) or independent (built directly from source systems). Data marts promote user autonomy and provide a scalable approach to data warehousing.

16. What is the difference between OLTP and OLAP systems?
Answer: OLTP (Online Transaction Processing) systems handle real-time transaction data and are optimized for speed and reliability in data entry, updates, and retrieval operations. They support day-to-day operations like banking, order processing, and inventory management. OLAP (Online Analytical Processing) systems, on the other hand, are designed for complex queries, data analysis, and historical data exploration. OLTP systems are normalized for consistency and speed, whereas OLAP systems are denormalized or multidimensional for analytical efficiency. OLTP supports operational tasks; OLAP supports strategic decision-making.

17. What are the key components of a data warehouse architecture?
Answer: A typical data warehouse architecture includes the following components:
Data Sources – operational systems, external files, etc.
ETL Process – tools to extract, transform, and load data.
Staging Area – temporary storage during ETL processing.
Data Storage – central repository (data warehouse) using relational or multidimensional models.
Metadata Repository – holds information about data structure and lineage.
Data Marts – specialized subsets for departmental use.
Access Tools – reporting, dashboard, and OLAP tools for end-users.
These components work together to ensure reliable data integration, storage, and analysis.

18. What is data cleansing and why is it important in data warehousing?
Answer: Data cleansing is the process of detecting and correcting errors or inconsistencies in data to improve its quality. It includes removing duplicates, standardizing formats, correcting inaccurate values, and handling missing data. In a data warehouse, where data from multiple sources is integrated, cleansing is crucial to ensure consistency and reliability. Poor data quality can lead to incorrect insights and flawed decision-making. Clean data enhances the performance of data mining and analytical tools, ensuring the warehouse serves as a trustworthy source for business intelligence.

19. What is a dimension hierarchy in OLAP systems?
Answer: A dimension hierarchy in OLAP systems is a structured organization of data levels within a dimension, allowing users to analyze data from general to detailed views. For example, a time dimension may have hierarchy levels like Year > Quarter > Month > Day. Hierarchies enable operations like drill-down and roll-up in OLAP, supporting flexible and intuitive data analysis. They also help in aggregating data at different levels, improving performance and user experience during multidimensional exploration of the data warehouse.

20. What is the purpose of indexing in data warehouses?
Answer: Indexing in data warehouses improves the speed and efficiency of query processing by enabling faster data retrieval. Since data warehouses handle large volumes of data and complex queries, appropriate indexing strategies are essential. Common index types include bitmap indexes and B-trees. Bitmap indexes are particularly effective in low-cardinality columns like gender or status. Indexes reduce the amount of data scanned during query execution, enhance join performance, and support aggregations. Proper indexing ensures that analytical queries perform optimally without unnecessary delay.

21. What are association rules in data mining?
Answer: Association rules are used in data mining to uncover interesting relationships and correlations between

variables in large datasets. One of the most popular applications is market basket analysis, where rules like "If a customer buys bread, they are likely to buy butter" are identified. Each rule is evaluated using support, confidence, and lift metrics. These rules help businesses understand consumer behavior, create recommendation systems, and optimize product placement. Association rules are foundational in discovering hidden patterns that may not be immediately obvious.

22. What is clustering in data mining?
Answer: Clustering is an unsupervised learning technique used in data mining to group similar data objects into clusters based on defined similarity metrics. Unlike classification, clustering does not require predefined labels. Algorithms like K-means, DBSCAN, and hierarchical clustering are commonly used. Applications include customer segmentation, anomaly detection, and document categorization. Clustering helps uncover natural groupings in data, making it easier to analyze and interpret large datasets by identifying patterns and trends without prior knowledge of group identities.

23. What is classification in data mining?
Answer: Classification is a supervised learning technique in data mining used to assign predefined labels to new data instances based on patterns learned from labeled training data. Common algorithms include Decision Trees, Naïve Bayes, Support Vector Machines, and Neural Networks. Applications of classification include spam detection, credit scoring, medical diagnosis, and customer churn prediction. The goal is to build models that can accurately predict the class of unseen data, aiding in decision-making and automation.

24. What is regression analysis in data mining?
Answer: Regression analysis is used in data mining to predict a continuous numeric value based on relationships between input variables. It identifies the strength and nature of relationships between dependent and independent variables. Linear regression is the most common method, though others like logistic regression and polynomial regression are also used. Applications include sales forecasting, risk analysis, and price prediction. Regression helps organizations make data-driven predictions by modeling and quantifying trends in data.

25. What is anomaly detection in data mining?
Answer: Anomaly detection, also known as outlier detection, involves identifying data points that deviate significantly from the normal pattern of a dataset. These anomalies may indicate rare but important events such as fraud, network intrusions, or equipment failures. Techniques used include statistical methods, clustering, and machine learning models like Isolation Forests. Anomaly detection is critical in applications where early identification of unusual behavior can prevent major losses or issues, enhancing security, quality control, and reliability in various domains.

26. What is the K-means clustering algorithm in data mining?
Answer: K-means is a popular clustering algorithm used in data mining to partition a dataset into K distinct, non-overlapping clusters. The algorithm starts by selecting K initial centroids randomly. It then assigns each data point to the nearest centroid based on distance (typically Euclidean distance) and recalculates the centroids based on the average of points in each cluster. This process repeats iteratively until the centroids stabilize or a maximum number of iterations is reached. K-means is efficient and easy to implement, making it suitable for large datasets. However, it requires the number of clusters to be predefined and may converge to local optima.

27. What is data transformation in the ETL process?
Answer: Data transformation is a phase in the ETL (Extract, Transform, Load) process where extracted data from various sources is converted into a suitable format for analysis or loading into a data warehouse. This includes tasks such as data cleaning, standardization, aggregation, encoding, filtering, and joining. Transformation ensures consistency, removes redundancies, and aligns data with the target schema. It plays a critical role in integrating heterogeneous data sources and preparing clean, reliable datasets for downstream reporting and analysis. Without proper transformation, data inconsistencies can lead to incorrect insights and poor decision-making.

28. What is a star schema in data warehousing?
Answer: A star schema is a widely used data warehouse schema design where a central fact table is connected to multiple dimension tables. The fact table contains quantitative data for analysis (e.g., sales, profit), while the dimension tables provide descriptive context (e.g., product, customer, time). The structure resembles a star, with the fact table at the center and dimension tables radiating outward. Star schema is simple, supports fast query performance,

and is easy for users to understand. It is especially useful in OLAP applications where high-speed aggregations and slicing/dicing of data are required.

29. What is a snowflake schema and how does it differ from a star schema?
Answer: A snowflake schema is a normalized form of a star schema where dimension tables are further split into additional tables, creating a hierarchy of dimension tables. This reduces data redundancy but increases the complexity of queries due to multiple joins. For example, a location dimension may be broken into separate tables for country, state, and city. In contrast, a star schema keeps dimension data denormalized for simplicity and faster access. While snowflake schemas save storage and maintain better data integrity, star schemas generally offer better performance for analytical queries.

30. What is a fact table and what does it store?
Answer: A fact table is the central table in a data warehouse schema that stores measurable, quantitative data for analysis, such as sales, revenue, or cost. It also contains foreign keys that reference dimension tables, allowing users to analyze facts across different dimensions like time, product, or region. Fact tables can be categorized as transaction fact tables (detailed, event-level data), snapshot fact tables (periodic data snapshots), or accumulating fact tables (cumulative data over a lifecycle). The structure of the fact table is crucial for query performance and analytical flexibility in a data warehouse environment.

31. What is data granularity in a data warehouse?
Answer: Data granularity refers to the level of detail or summarization of data stored in a data warehouse. Fine granularity means data is stored at a very detailed level (e.g., individual sales transactions), while coarse granularity refers to summarized data (e.g., monthly or yearly totals). The choice of granularity impacts storage, performance, and analysis. Fine-grained data allows detailed analysis but requires more storage and may slow performance. Coarse-grained data offers faster queries but may limit drill-down capabilities. Many warehouses store both granular and summarized data to balance flexibility and efficiency.

32. What are the major types of data in data mining?
Answer: Data in data mining can be broadly categorized into the following types:
Structured Data – Data organized in rows and columns (e.g., relational databases).
Semi-Structured Data – Data with some structure but not rigidly formatted (e.g., XML, JSON).
Unstructured Data – Data without a predefined format (e.g., text, images, videos).
Time-Series Data – Data collected over time intervals (e.g., stock prices, sensor data).
Spatial Data – Data related to space or geography (e.g., maps, satellite images).
Each type presents unique challenges and opportunities in data mining and may require different preprocessing and analysis techniques.

33. What is data discretization in data preprocessing?
Answer: Data discretization is the process of converting continuous numerical data into categorical or discrete intervals. It simplifies data, reduces the number of distinct values, and can enhance the performance of certain machine learning algorithms like decision trees. Discretization techniques include equal-width binning, equal-frequency binning, and clustering-based methods. It is particularly useful in classification tasks where categorical inputs are required. While discretization can help highlight meaningful patterns, improper binning can lead to loss of information or misleading patterns, so it must be done carefully.

34. What is web mining and what are its types?
Answer: Web mining refers to the application of data mining techniques to discover patterns and knowledge from web data. It is categorized into three types:
Web Content Mining – Analyzes the content of web pages (text, images, videos).
Web Structure Mining – Examines the structure of hyperlinks between documents.
Web Usage Mining – Studies user interaction data, such as clickstreams and server logs.
Web mining helps in areas like personalization, recommendation systems, and improving user experience. It plays a vital role in e-commerce, digital marketing, and online analytics.

35. What is the purpose of normalization in data preprocessing?
Answer: Normalization in data preprocessing refers to scaling data to a standard range, typically between 0 and 1 or -

1 and 1. It ensures that features contribute equally to the model, especially when they have different units or scales. Common normalization methods include min-max normalization, z-score standardization, and decimal scaling. Normalization is essential for distance-based algorithms like K-means or k-NN, as large-scale variables can dominate smaller ones, skewing results. It enhances model performance, convergence speed, and the reliability of predictions.

36. What is a decision tree in data mining?
Answer: A decision tree is a supervised learning algorithm used for classification and regression tasks. It represents decisions and their possible outcomes in a tree-like structure. Each internal node denotes a test on an attribute, each branch represents the outcome of the test, and each leaf node represents a class label or result. Algorithms like ID3, C4.5, and CART are commonly used to construct decision trees. They are easy to interpret, handle both numerical and categorical data, and work well with large datasets, making them a popular choice in data mining applications.

37. What is pruning in decision trees?
Answer: Pruning is a technique used in decision trees to reduce overfitting and improve generalization by removing branches that have little predictive power. There are two types of pruning:
Pre-pruning (early stopping) – Stops tree construction early based on criteria like depth or minimum samples per node.
Post-pruning – Removes branches from a fully grown tree using validation data.
Pruning simplifies the model, reduces complexity, and enhances accuracy on unseen data. It is crucial for preventing over-complex trees that perform well on training data but poorly on new data.

38. What is entropy in data mining?
Answer: Entropy is a measure of impurity or randomness used in decision tree algorithms to determine the best attribute for splitting data. It quantifies the uncertainty or disorder in a dataset. A lower entropy indicates more homogeneous data, while higher entropy means more diversity. The goal in constructing a decision tree is to reduce entropy at each split, thereby creating more informative and pure subsets. Entropy is used alongside information gain to select attributes that provide the most significant reduction in uncertainty.

39. What is information gain in data mining?
Answer: Information gain measures the reduction in entropy achieved by splitting a dataset based on a particular attribute. It helps identify the attribute that best separates the data into distinct classes. Information gain is calculated as the difference between the entropy of the original dataset and the weighted average entropy of the subsets created by the split. The attribute with the highest information gain is chosen for splitting. This principle is widely used in decision tree algorithms like ID3 and C4.5 to build accurate and efficient models.

40. What is lift in association rule mining?
Answer: Lift is a measure used to evaluate the strength of an association rule in data mining. It is the ratio of the observed support of a rule to the expected support if the antecedent and consequent were independent. Mathematically, lift = confidence / expected confidence. A lift value greater than 1 indicates a positive correlation between items, meaning they occur together more often than expected. A lift of 1 means no correlation, and less than 1 implies a negative correlation. Lift helps identify strong and useful associations in large datasets.

41. What is OLAP in data warehousing?
Answer: Online Analytical Processing (OLAP) is a category of data processing that enables users to interactively analyze multidimensional data from multiple perspectives. OLAP allows complex queries and computations such as trend analysis, slice and dice, drill-down, and pivoting across dimensions like time, geography, and product. It uses structures like data cubes to organize data, enabling fast and flexible analysis. OLAP systems are typically categorized into ROLAP (Relational OLAP), MOLAP (Multidimensional OLAP), and HOLAP (Hybrid OLAP). OLAP plays a key role in decision support systems and business intelligence applications.

42. What is ROLAP and how does it differ from MOLAP?
Answer: ROLAP (Relational OLAP) is a type of OLAP that stores data in relational databases and performs analysis using complex SQL queries. It is suitable for large datasets and supports scalability, but may be slower in performance compared to MOLAP. MOLAP (Multidimensional OLAP) stores data in multidimensional cubes, allowing faster query execution and real-time analysis. However, MOLAP may suffer from data volume limitations and pre-processing overhead. ROLAP is better for detailed data with frequent updates, while MOLAP is ideal for summarized data with high performance needs.

43. What is data mart and how is it different from a data warehouse?

Answer: A data mart is a subset of a data warehouse that is focused on a specific business area, such as sales, finance, or marketing. It is designed to serve the needs of a particular department or group of users. Data marts are smaller, faster to deploy, and easier to manage than enterprise-wide data warehouses. While a data warehouse integrates data from across the organization for comprehensive analysis, data marts provide focused, domain-specific insights. They can be dependent (sourced from a central warehouse) or independent (sourced directly from operational systems).

44. What is the difference between OLTP and OLAP systems?

Answer: OLTP (Online Transaction Processing) systems are designed for managing day-to-day transactional data, such as order processing or banking transactions. They focus on fast insert, update, and delete operations and ensure data integrity in high-concurrency environments. OLAP (Online Analytical Processing) systems, on the other hand, are used for analytical queries on historical data to support decision-making. They emphasize read-intensive operations, complex queries, and data summarization. In essence, OLTP is optimized for data entry and retrieval, while OLAP is optimized for data analysis.

45. What is metadata in data warehousing?

Answer: Metadata in data warehousing refers to data about data. It provides descriptive information about the structure, operations, origin, and usage of the data stored in the warehouse. Metadata helps users and systems understand where data comes from, how it's transformed, and how it should be interpreted. It is categorized into technical metadata (schemas, data types), business metadata (definitions, rules), and operational metadata (ETL logs, load times). Metadata enhances data governance, traceability, and usability, making it a critical component of any data warehousing system.

46. What is data profiling and why is it important?

Answer: Data profiling is the process of analyzing data to understand its structure, quality, and content. It involves examining data types, distributions, patterns, missing values, and relationships. Profiling helps detect anomalies, inconsistencies, and potential data quality issues before data is used in analytics or loaded into a data warehouse. It is crucial for building reliable data pipelines, ensuring data integrity, and supporting accurate decision-making. Data profiling tools automate much of this analysis and are commonly used during the data integration and cleansing stages.

47. What are surrogate keys and why are they used in data warehouses?

Answer: Surrogate keys are artificial, system-generated identifiers used to uniquely identify records in dimension tables of a data warehouse. Unlike natural keys, surrogate keys have no business meaning and are typically integers. They simplify joins between fact and dimension tables, support slowly changing dimensions, and help maintain historical data consistency. Surrogate keys avoid problems associated with changing natural keys and allow for better performance and indexing in large datasets. They are a best practice in dimensional modeling for robust data warehousing.

48. What is the ETL testing process?

Answer: ETL testing involves validating the Extract, Transform, and Load processes to ensure data is correctly extracted from source systems, accurately transformed according to business rules, and properly loaded into the data warehouse. The testing process includes source-to-target data validation, transformation logic verification, data completeness checks, data quality checks, and performance testing. ETL testing ensures data integrity, accuracy, and reliability before it is used for reporting and analysis. It is essential for building trust in data and supporting critical business decisions.

49. What is clustering in data mining and what are its applications?

Answer: Clustering is an unsupervised learning technique used to group similar data points into clusters based on similarity measures such as distance. Unlike classification, clustering does not rely on predefined labels. Common algorithms include K-means, DBSCAN, and hierarchical clustering. Applications of clustering include customer segmentation, market research, anomaly detection, image processing, and social network analysis. Clustering helps discover hidden patterns and natural groupings in data, enabling better targeting and personalization in various industries.

50. What is data warehouse partitioning and what are its benefits?
Answer: Data warehouse partitioning involves dividing large fact tables into smaller, more manageable segments called partitions based on criteria like date, region, or product category. Partitioning improves query performance by reducing the amount of data scanned during analysis. It also enhances data maintenance by enabling operations like loading, archiving, or purging to be performed on individual partitions. There are different types of partitioning, such as range, list, and hash partitioning. Partitioning helps in optimizing storage, increasing scalability, and simplifying data management in large-scale data warehouses.

51. What is star schema in data warehouse design?
Answer: A star schema is a type of dimensional model used in data warehouse design. It consists of a central fact table that stores quantitative data (measures) and is connected to multiple dimension tables that contain descriptive attributes. The structure resembles a star, with the fact table at the center and the dimension tables radiating outward. Star schema is simple, easy to understand, and optimizes query performance. It supports fast aggregation and slicing-and-dicing operations, making it ideal for OLAP and decision support systems.

52. What is snowflake schema and how does it differ from star schema?
Answer: A snowflake schema is a variation of the star schema where dimension tables are normalized into multiple related tables. This results in a more complex structure resembling a snowflake. While star schemas offer faster query performance due to denormalized dimensions, snowflake schemas improve data integrity and reduce redundancy by organizing attributes into sub-dimensions. Snowflake schemas are suitable when storage optimization and normalization are priorities, but they may increase query complexity and require more joins during data retrieval.

53. What is a conformed dimension in data warehousing?
Answer: A conformed dimension is a dimension that is shared across multiple fact tables or data marts within a data warehouse. It maintains consistent meaning and structure, allowing data to be compared and analyzed across different subject areas. For example, a conformed "Customer" dimension can be used in both sales and support fact tables. Conformed dimensions promote data consistency, facilitate integrated reporting, and simplify ETL processes by avoiding duplication and inconsistencies.

54. What are slowly changing dimensions (SCD)?
Answer: Slowly Changing Dimensions (SCD) are dimensions in a data warehouse where attribute values change slowly over time. SCDs are managed using different techniques to preserve historical data or update values. The common types are: Type 1 (overwrite old data), Type 2 (store new version with timestamp), and Type 3 (track limited history using additional columns). Handling SCDs is crucial for maintaining accurate historical reporting and understanding how data evolves over time.

55. What is dimensional modeling and why is it important?
Answer: Dimensional modeling is a data design technique used in data warehouses to optimize for analytical querying. It organizes data into fact and dimension tables in schemas such as star or snowflake. The goal is to make data intuitive, performant, and easy to navigate for business users. Dimensional modeling supports fast aggregation, historical analysis, and reporting. It is important because it aligns technical design with business needs, enabling efficient and user-friendly analytics.

56. What is data redundancy and how is it handled in a data warehouse?
Answer: Data redundancy refers to the unnecessary duplication of data within a database or data warehouse. While some redundancy is acceptable in dimensional models (e.g., denormalized dimension tables for performance), excessive redundancy can lead to inconsistencies, increased storage costs, and maintenance challenges. It is handled by normalization (where appropriate), using surrogate keys, applying data deduplication techniques during ETL, and maintaining a single source of truth through master data management.

57. What are factless fact tables?
Answer: Factless fact tables are fact tables that do not contain measurable numeric data but instead capture events or conditions. They are used to record occurrences such as student attendance, employee absences, or product promotions. Factless fact tables help answer "what happened" or "what did not happen" questions by linking dimension tables without containing traditional facts. They are useful for tracking events, managing many-to-many relationships, and performing conditional analysis.

58. What is a hybrid schema in data warehousing?
Answer: A hybrid schema in data warehousing combines features of both star and snowflake schemas. It uses denormalized dimensions like a star schema for performance, while also normalizing some dimensions as in a snowflake schema for data integrity. Hybrid schemas offer a balance between performance and maintainability. They are often adopted in large-scale data warehouses where some dimensions benefit from normalization without compromising query speed significantly.

59. What is a data lake and how does it differ from a data warehouse?
Answer: A data lake is a centralized repository that stores structured, semi-structured, and unstructured data at scale. It uses flat architecture and stores raw data without predefined schemas. In contrast, a data warehouse stores structured, processed data optimized for querying and reporting. Data lakes support flexible analytics, big data processing, and machine learning, while data warehouses are best suited for business intelligence and structured reporting. Both can coexist in modern data architectures for different analytical needs.

60. What is the role of Apache Hive in data warehousing?
Answer: Apache Hive is a data warehousing tool built on top of Hadoop that enables querying and analyzing large datasets using SQL-like HiveQL language. It translates queries into MapReduce or other execution engines like Tez or Spark. Hive supports structured data, schema management, and integration with BI tools. It is widely used in big data environments to perform data summarization, ad hoc queries, and analysis on massive volumes of data stored in HDFS or cloud storage.

61. What is the purpose of a data cube in OLAP?
Answer: A data cube is a multidimensional array of values used in OLAP to represent data across multiple dimensions such as time, location, and product. It allows users to perform complex analytical operations like slicing, dicing, roll-up, and drill-down efficiently. Data cubes enhance performance by pre-aggregating data and storing it in optimized formats. They enable intuitive navigation and interactive analysis, making them valuable tools in decision support and business intelligence systems.

62. What is a surrogate key and how does it help with slowly changing dimensions?
Answer: A surrogate key is a system-generated unique identifier used in dimension tables. It replaces natural keys to improve data integrity and simplify relationships. In slowly changing dimensions (SCD Type 2), surrogate keys are essential for tracking multiple versions of records. When a dimension attribute changes, a new record is inserted with a new surrogate key, preserving historical data. This helps in maintaining accurate historical analysis and version control in the data warehouse.

63. What is the role of an ETL scheduler in data warehousing?
Answer: An ETL scheduler is a tool or component that automates the execution of ETL jobs at predefined intervals. It ensures that data extraction, transformation, and loading processes run at the right time without manual intervention. ETL schedulers support dependencies, error handling, notifications, and logging. They are critical for maintaining data freshness, coordinating data workflows, and ensuring that data is consistently available for reporting and analysis.

64. What is normalization and why is it avoided in dimensional modeling?
Answer: Normalization is the process of organizing data to eliminate redundancy and improve data integrity by splitting data into multiple related tables. In dimensional modeling, normalization is often avoided to simplify queries and improve performance. Denormalized dimension tables reduce the need for complex joins, resulting in faster query execution. While normalized schemas are ideal for OLTP systems, dimensional models prioritize readability and speed for OLAP and reporting purposes.

65. What are hierarchies in dimension tables and how are they used?
Answer: Hierarchies in dimension tables define logical relationships between attributes, such as Country > State > City or Year > Quarter > Month. They enable users to navigate data at different levels of granularity through drill-down and roll-up operations in OLAP tools. Hierarchies support grouping, summarization, and filtering of data in meaningful ways, enhancing the analytical capabilities of data warehouses. They are a key feature in dimensional modeling and reporting.

66. What is the significance of data integration in data warehousing?
Answer: Data integration is the process of combining data from multiple sources into a unified view. In data warehousing, it ensures that data from various operational systems is harmonized, cleansed, and transformed into a consistent format for analysis. Integration involves resolving data conflicts, standardizing formats, and removing duplicates. Effective data integration improves data quality, supports comprehensive analysis, and enables informed decision-making across the organization.

67. What are the benefits of data cleansing in ETL?
Answer: Data cleansing is the process of detecting and correcting errors, inconsistencies, and inaccuracies in data. During ETL, cleansing improves data quality by removing duplicates, standardizing formats, correcting missing values, and validating business rules. Benefits include more accurate analytics, better decision-making, compliance with data standards, and increased trust in the data. Cleansed data enhances user confidence and ensures reliable business intelligence outcomes.

68. What is a schema-on-write vs. schema-on-read?
Answer: Schema-on-write is a data storage approach where the schema is defined before data is written to the database, as seen in traditional data warehouses. It enforces structure and validation upfront. Schema-on-read, used in data lakes, stores data in raw form and applies structure only when the data is read for analysis. This provides flexibility in handling diverse data formats but may involve complex transformation during retrieval. The choice depends on use case, governance needs, and performance requirements.

69. What is data lineage and why is it important?
Answer: Data lineage describes the lifecycle of data, including its origin, transformations, and movement across systems. It provides a traceable path from source to destination, helping users understand how data has changed over time. Data lineage is crucial for debugging, impact analysis, auditing, and regulatory compliance. It ensures transparency, enhances data governance, and supports trust in data-driven processes within a data warehouse environment.

70. What is predictive modeling in data mining?
Answer: Predictive modeling is a data mining technique used to forecast future outcomes based on historical data. It uses statistical and machine learning algorithms such as regression, decision trees, and neural networks to identify patterns and relationships. Predictive models are applied in areas like customer churn prediction, credit scoring, and demand forecasting. They enable businesses to make proactive, data-driven decisions and improve strategic planning.

71. What is the purpose of OLAP in data warehousing?
Answer: The purpose of OLAP (Online Analytical Processing) in data warehousing is to enable users to perform multidimensional analysis of large volumes of data. OLAP tools allow for complex calculations, trend analysis, and data modeling through operations like slicing, dicing, drilling down, and rolling up. It supports business intelligence by providing fast and interactive access to aggregated data across different dimensions, helping users derive insights and make informed decisions.

72. What is the difference between ETL and ELT?
Answer: ETL (Extract, Transform, Load) involves extracting data from sources, transforming it into the required format, and then loading it into the data warehouse. ELT (Extract, Load, Transform), on the other hand, loads raw data into the warehouse first and then performs transformations within the warehouse using its processing power. ELT is common in modern cloud-based data warehouses that can handle complex transformations efficiently post-loading.

73. What are KPIs in a data warehouse and why are they important?
Answer: KPIs (Key Performance Indicators) are quantifiable metrics used to evaluate the success of an organization or a particular activity. In a data warehouse, KPIs are derived from the fact tables and are used in dashboards and reports to measure performance against strategic goals. They are important because they provide actionable insights, help track progress, and support data-driven decision-making across departments and levels of management.

74. What is data granularity in data warehousing?
Answer: Data granularity refers to the level of detail or summarization in the data stored within a data warehouse. High granularity means detailed data (e.g., individual transactions), while low granularity refers to summarized or

aggregated data (e.g., daily or monthly totals). Managing granularity is essential for balancing storage efficiency, query performance, and analytical needs. Properly chosen granularity ensures meaningful insights without overwhelming users with excessive detail.

75. What is data profiling and how does it help in ETL?
Answer: Data profiling is the process of analyzing data to understand its structure, quality, and content. It involves assessing data types, patterns, null values, duplicates, and inconsistencies. In ETL, data profiling helps identify data quality issues early, informs transformation logic, and ensures accurate and clean data is loaded into the warehouse. It also supports compliance, metadata management, and the creation of robust data integration processes.

76. How does metadata management benefit data warehousing?
Answer: Metadata management involves maintaining information about data definitions, origins, usage, and structures. In data warehousing, it helps users understand the context and meaning of data, supports lineage tracking, and ensures consistency across ETL processes. Effective metadata management enhances data governance, improves user trust, simplifies troubleshooting, and provides documentation that supports the long-term sustainability of the data warehouse environment.

77. What is data staging in ETL?
Answer: Data staging is the temporary storage area used during the ETL process where extracted data is placed before transformation and loading into the data warehouse. It acts as a buffer zone where data is cleansed, validated, and transformed. Staging helps isolate data processing, reduces load on source systems, and allows for troubleshooting and data reconciliation. It also ensures that only clean and consistent data enters the warehouse.

78. What are fact tables and dimension tables?
Answer: Fact tables contain the measurable, quantitative data such as sales, revenue, or transactions. They typically include foreign keys to dimension tables and numeric facts. Dimension tables contain descriptive attributes (e.g., customer name, date, product category) used to slice and dice data in analysis. Fact tables support aggregation and analytics, while dimension tables provide context to the measures, enabling business insights through multi-dimensional reporting.

79. What is the role of indexes in data warehousing?
Answer: Indexes in data warehousing improve the speed and efficiency of data retrieval operations. They help the query engine quickly locate rows in large tables without scanning the entire dataset. Indexes are especially useful for frequently queried columns, join conditions, and filters in OLAP environments. However, they must be used judiciously, as too many indexes can slow down data loading and increase storage requirements.

80. What is data auditing in the context of data warehousing?
Answer: Data auditing involves tracking and verifying the accuracy, completeness, and integrity of data as it moves through the ETL process and into the data warehouse. It ensures that data transformations are performed correctly, and that source-to-target mappings are accurate. Data auditing provides a historical trail of data modifications and is essential for compliance, troubleshooting, and building user trust in analytical outcomes.

81. What is a data mart and how does it differ from a data warehouse?
Answer: A data mart is a subset of a data warehouse that is focused on a specific business area such as sales, finance, or marketing. While a data warehouse integrates data from across the entire organization, a data mart is typically department-specific and optimized for that team's reporting needs. Data marts can be dependent (sourced from the data warehouse) or independent (sourced directly from operational systems), offering quicker access and simpler structures for end-users.

82. What is the role of data wrangling in data preparation?
Answer: Data wrangling, also known as data munging, is the process of cleaning, transforming, and organizing raw data into a usable format for analysis. It includes handling missing values, formatting inconsistencies, merging datasets, and removing outliers. Data wrangling is crucial in data preparation as it improves data quality and ensures that analytical models and reports are based on accurate, consistent, and complete datasets.

83. What is association rule mining?
Answer: Association rule mining is a data mining technique used to discover interesting relationships and patterns between variables in large datasets. It is commonly used in market basket analysis to find items that frequently co-occur in transactions. Rules are evaluated using support, confidence, and lift metrics. For example, the rule {bread, butter} → {jam} indicates that customers buying bread and butter often buy jam as well. This technique aids in cross-selling and recommendation systems.

84. What is classification in data mining?
Answer: Classification is a supervised learning technique in data mining used to categorize data into predefined classes or labels. It involves training a model on a labeled dataset and using it to predict the class of new data points. Common algorithms include decision trees, logistic regression, support vector machines, and neural networks. Classification is widely used in spam detection, credit scoring, medical diagnosis, and customer segmentation.

85. What is clustering in data mining?
Answer: Clustering is an unsupervised learning technique used to group similar data points into clusters based on their attributes. Unlike classification, clustering does not rely on predefined labels. Algorithms like k-means, hierarchical clustering, and DBSCAN are used to identify patterns and natural groupings in the data. Clustering is useful in customer segmentation, anomaly detection, and organizing large datasets into meaningful structures for further analysis.

86. What is the importance of data quality in data mining?
Answer: Data quality is critical in data mining because the accuracy, completeness, and consistency of data directly influence the reliability of mining results. Poor data quality can lead to incorrect patterns, misleading predictions, and flawed business decisions. High-quality data ensures meaningful insights, better model performance, and greater user trust. Ensuring data quality involves cleansing, validation, standardization, and continuous monitoring throughout the data lifecycle.

87. What is web mining and its applications?
Answer: Web mining is the process of extracting useful information and knowledge from web data, including web content, structure, and usage logs. It is categorized into web content mining, web structure mining, and web usage mining. Applications include personalized recommendations, website optimization, user behavior analysis, and targeted marketing. Web mining helps businesses understand customer preferences and enhance digital experiences.

88. What are decision trees and how are they used in data mining?
Answer: Decision trees are a popular data mining technique used for classification and regression tasks. They split data into subsets based on feature values, creating a tree-like structure of decisions. Each internal node represents a condition, and each leaf node represents a class label or outcome. Decision trees are easy to interpret, handle both numerical and categorical data, and support feature selection. They are widely used in risk assessment, diagnostics, and customer profiling.

89. What is the role of neural networks in data mining?
Answer: Neural networks are machine learning models inspired by the human brain's structure, capable of learning complex patterns in large datasets. In data mining, they are used for tasks like classification, regression, and pattern recognition. They consist of layers of interconnected nodes (neurons) that adjust weights through training. Neural networks excel in processing unstructured data such as images, text, and audio and are foundational to deep learning applications.

90. What is data visualization and why is it important in data mining?
Answer: Data visualization is the graphical representation of data and analytical results through charts, graphs, and dashboards. It is important in data mining because it helps users understand patterns, trends, and outliers in data more effectively than raw tables. Visualization supports exploratory analysis, decision-making, and communication of insights to stakeholders. Tools like Tableau, Power BI, and matplotlib are commonly used for data visualization.

91. What is anomaly detection in data mining?
Answer: Anomaly detection is the process of identifying rare or unusual data points that differ significantly from the majority of the dataset. These anomalies may indicate critical incidents such as fraud, network intrusions, or medical

issues. Techniques like statistical methods, clustering, and machine learning are used for anomaly detection. It plays a vital role in security systems, financial monitoring, and system health diagnostics.

92. What is the use of dimensional reduction in data mining?
Answer: Dimensional reduction is used to reduce the number of variables or features in a dataset while retaining the most important information. Techniques like Principal Component Analysis (PCA) and t-SNE help in simplifying data, removing noise, and improving model performance. It also enhances visualization and reduces the risk of overfitting. Dimensional reduction is essential for handling high-dimensional data efficiently.

93. What is the purpose of a star schema in data warehousing?
Answer: A star schema is a database schema design used in data warehousing that organizes data into fact and dimension tables. The fact table is at the center and is connected to multiple dimension tables in a star-like structure. This design simplifies queries and improves performance in OLAP systems by reducing joins. It is widely used due to its simplicity and efficiency in analytical processing.

94. What are surrogate keys in data warehouses?
Answer: Surrogate keys are unique identifiers used in data warehouses in place of natural keys. They are typically system-generated integers that act as primary keys in dimension tables. Surrogate keys provide consistency, simplify joins, and improve performance. They also allow for better handling of slowly changing dimensions, ensuring historical accuracy and data integrity over time.

95. What is the snowflake schema and how does it differ from a star schema?
Answer: A snowflake schema is a more normalized version of the star schema, where dimension tables are broken down into sub-dimension tables. This design reduces data redundancy and storage space but may require more complex queries due to additional joins. While star schema is preferred for faster performance and simplicity, snowflake schema is used when normalization and storage efficiency are prioritized.

96. What is incremental loading in ETL processes?
Answer: Incremental loading refers to the technique of loading only new or changed data from the source into the data warehouse during each ETL cycle. This method improves efficiency by avoiding the reprocessing of unchanged data. Techniques such as timestamp comparison, change data capture (CDC), and log-based replication are commonly used. Incremental loading reduces processing time and system load, especially with large datasets.

97. What are data mining tools and give examples?
Answer: Data mining tools are software applications used to discover patterns, relationships, and trends in large datasets. These tools offer functionalities such as classification, clustering, regression, and association rule mining. Examples include RapidMiner, KNIME, Weka, Orange, SAS Enterprise Miner, and IBM SPSS Modeler. These tools help data scientists and analysts automate data mining tasks and generate valuable insights efficiently.

98. What is the importance of data integration in data warehousing?
Answer: Data integration is crucial in data warehousing as it involves combining data from multiple heterogeneous sources into a unified view. It ensures consistency, accuracy, and completeness of data across the enterprise. Integration enables comprehensive analysis, supports business intelligence, and facilitates better decision-making. Techniques include ETL processes, middleware solutions, and data virtualization.

99. What are slowly changing dimensions (SCD) and their types?
Answer: Slowly Changing Dimensions (SCD) refer to dimension data that changes slowly over time rather than frequently. There are mainly three types:
Type 1: Overwrites old data (no history maintained)
Type 2: Adds a new row with a new surrogate key to preserve history
Type 3: Adds a new column to track the previous value
Handling SCDs correctly is vital for maintaining historical accuracy in the data warehouse.

100. What is the CRISP-DM methodology in data mining?
Answer: CRISP-DM (Cross Industry Standard Process for Data Mining) is a widely used methodology that provides a structured approach to data mining projects. It consists of six phases: Business Understanding, Data Understanding,

Data Preparation, Modeling, Evaluation, and Deployment. CRISP-DM helps ensure that data mining efforts align with business objectives and follow a systematic, repeatable, and effective process for generating actionable insights.

101. What are the key components of data warehouse architecture?
Answer: A data warehouse architecture typically includes several key components: data sources, ETL (Extract, Transform, Load) tools, a central data warehouse, metadata, and front-end tools. Data sources may include operational databases, flat files, or external data. ETL tools extract data, clean and transform it into a suitable format, and load it into the warehouse. The central data repository stores integrated, subject-oriented, time-variant, and non-volatile data. Metadata describes the data warehouse structure, contents, and rules. Finally, front-end tools enable users to query, analyze, and report data. These components work together to support effective decision-making and business intelligence.

102. What is the difference between dependent and independent data marts?
Answer: Dependent data marts derive data from a central data warehouse and thus ensure consistency across business units. They are easier to manage, support integrated analysis, and follow a standardized data model. Independent data marts, on the other hand, are standalone systems built directly from operational or external data sources. They are quicker to implement but may result in data silos and inconsistencies. The choice depends on the organization's size, budget, and integration needs. Dependent data marts are preferred in large enterprises requiring unified reporting, while independent marts may suit smaller, departmental applications.

103. What is the role of metadata in a data warehouse?
Answer: Metadata plays a crucial role in data warehouses by providing context, structure, and meaning to the stored data. It describes data sources, transformation rules, data models, data types, data lineage, and user access. Metadata facilitates efficient navigation, data governance, and query optimization. It also supports ETL processes by guiding data mapping and transformation. There are two types: technical metadata, used by developers and administrators, and business metadata, aimed at end users. Accurate metadata enhances usability, ensures data quality, and improves decision-making capabilities by helping users understand and trust the data.

104. How do OLTP and OLAP systems differ in functionality?
Answer: OLTP (Online Transaction Processing) systems manage day-to-day business transactions like order entry and inventory updates. They are optimized for insert, update, and delete operations with high concurrency and data consistency. OLAP (Online Analytical Processing) systems, on the other hand, are designed for complex queries, trend analysis, and decision support. They support multidimensional views of data and are optimized for read-heavy operations. OLTP is operational, dealing with current data, while OLAP is analytical, working with historical data. OLTP supports real-time business processes, whereas OLAP enables strategic business insights through data mining and analysis.

105. What is a conformed dimension in data warehousing?
Answer: A conformed dimension is a dimension that is consistent and standardized across multiple fact tables or data marts. It ensures that different data marts use the same attributes and definitions for analysis, allowing integrated reporting and comparison. For example, a "Time" dimension used in both sales and inventory data marts with the same date hierarchy is a conformed dimension. Using conformed dimensions promotes data consistency, simplifies ETL processes, and facilitates enterprise-wide business intelligence. They are essential for maintaining the integrity of a dimensional model and enabling drill-across analysis in reporting tools.

106. What is snowflake schema and how does it differ from star schema?
Answer: A snowflake schema is a type of dimensional model where dimension tables are normalized, breaking them into multiple related tables to reduce redundancy. This leads to a more complex structure with multiple joins, but improved data integrity. In contrast, a star schema keeps dimension tables denormalized and simple, offering faster query performance and ease of use. Snowflake schema is more storage-efficient but slower for queries due to additional joins. Star schema is preferred for user-friendly reporting, while snowflake schema may be used when storage or normalization is a priority.

107. What are surrogate keys and why are they used in data warehousing?
Answer: Surrogate keys are artificial or system-generated keys used to uniquely identify records in dimension tables. They are typically integers and are independent of the operational keys used in source systems. Surrogate keys provide

several benefits: they ensure uniqueness, allow historical tracking (slowly changing dimensions), and isolate data warehouse schema from changes in source systems. For example, if a customer's source key changes, the surrogate key ensures that historical data remains consistent. Surrogate keys also improve performance in joins and are a best practice in dimensional modeling.

108. What is the purpose of a factless fact table?
Answer: A factless fact table captures events or relationships between dimensions that do not have associated numerical measures. It is used to track the occurrence of events such as student attendance, product promotions, or employee leaves. Although it lacks traditional facts like sales or profit, it provides analytical value by allowing counts and presence-based queries. For example, counting how many students attended a class or how many times a promotion was active. Factless fact tables support business process tracking and help in deriving key performance indicators from non-measured data.

109. What is a star join optimization in data warehouse queries?
Answer: Star join optimization is a performance enhancement technique used by query optimizers in relational databases when dealing with star schema queries. It involves recognizing a join pattern between a central fact table and multiple dimension tables, and then restructuring the query execution plan to reduce computation. This might include bitmap indexing, join indexing, or materialized views. The goal is to minimize scan time, optimize memory usage, and accelerate response time for OLAP queries. Star join optimization is particularly useful in decision support systems with complex, multidimensional queries.

110. How is data quality ensured in data warehousing?
Answer: Ensuring data quality in a data warehouse involves multiple strategies such as data profiling, cleansing, validation, standardization, and monitoring. Data profiling helps identify anomalies and inconsistencies. Cleansing corrects errors and removes duplicates. Validation checks enforce rules like data type conformity, range checks, and referential integrity. Standardization brings uniformity in data representation, such as consistent date formats. Continuous monitoring and auditing detect new issues over time. Implementing a robust ETL process, establishing data governance policies, and using data quality tools all contribute to building a trustworthy and reliable data warehouse environment.

111. What is the purpose of an ETL process in data warehousing?
Answer: The ETL (Extract, Transform, Load) process is essential in data warehousing as it handles the movement and transformation of data from multiple source systems into a unified format for analysis. Extraction involves retrieving raw data from various databases, files, or external systems. Transformation applies business rules to cleanse, filter, map, or enrich the data to match the warehouse schema. Finally, loading inserts the processed data into the data warehouse. ETL ensures data quality, consistency, and readiness for analytical queries. A robust ETL system supports timely updates and helps maintain a reliable decision-support environment.

112. What are the benefits of using dimensional modeling in data warehouses?
Answer: Dimensional modeling offers several advantages for data warehousing, especially in simplifying data access and enhancing performance. It organizes data into fact and dimension tables, making it intuitive for users to understand and query. The structure supports fast query execution due to its optimized schema and indexing. Dimensional models are also flexible for slicing, dicing, drilling down, and rolling up data, aiding comprehensive analysis. Additionally, they provide consistency in reporting and are scalable for handling large datasets. This modeling approach forms the foundation of OLAP systems and business intelligence solutions.

113. What is the concept of slowly changing dimensions (SCD)?
Answer: Slowly Changing Dimensions (SCD) refer to dimension attributes that change infrequently over time but require historical tracking in data warehouses. For example, a customer changing their address. SCDs are categorized into types: Type 1 overwrites old data without retaining history; Type 2 creates a new row for every change to preserve history; Type 3 stores previous values in additional columns, useful for limited history. Managing SCDs is crucial to ensure accurate time-based analysis and reports. The appropriate type depends on business needs for historical tracking and system performance.

114. What is data granularity in a data warehouse?
Answer: Data granularity refers to the level of detail or summarization of data stored in the data warehouse. High

granularity means data is stored in its most detailed form (e.g., individual transactions), while low granularity implies summarized or aggregated data (e.g., daily or monthly totals). Determining the appropriate granularity is essential for balancing performance, storage, and analytical needs. Fine-grained data allows flexible analysis but requires more storage and processing. Coarse-grained data is faster to query but less versatile. Often, warehouses store data at multiple granularities for optimized access.

115. What are the major types of fact tables?
Answer: There are three primary types of fact tables in data warehousing:
Transactional Fact Table – records individual business transactions (e.g., sales).
Periodic Snapshot Fact Table – captures data at regular intervals (e.g., monthly balances).
Accumulating Snapshot Fact Table – tracks the progress of a process (e.g., order fulfillment).
Each type serves a distinct analytical purpose. Transactional tables provide detailed operational data, periodic snapshots support trend analysis, and accumulating snapshots monitor process performance. Choosing the right type depends on the business scenario and analysis goals.

116. What is data mining and how is it different from data warehousing?
Answer: Data mining is the process of discovering patterns, trends, correlations, or anomalies from large datasets using statistical, mathematical, and machine learning techniques. Its goal is to extract actionable knowledge from stored data. Data warehousing, on the other hand, is the infrastructure used to collect, store, and manage integrated data from various sources to support decision-making. While a data warehouse provides a consolidated platform for data storage and access, data mining derives insights from it. Essentially, warehousing prepares and organizes data, while mining analyzes and interprets it.

117. What is the role of OLAP in data mining?
Answer: OLAP (Online Analytical Processing) plays a supporting role in data mining by providing multidimensional views of data that are easy to explore and summarize. OLAP helps identify potential patterns, outliers, or areas of interest, which can then be further analyzed using advanced mining techniques. For example, OLAP can reveal a drop in sales for a product category in a region, prompting deeper mining for reasons such as customer churn or competitor activity. OLAP facilitates interactive exploration, while data mining delivers predictive and descriptive models from that data.

118. What is association rule mining in data mining?
Answer: Association rule mining is a data mining technique used to uncover interesting relationships or patterns between variables in large datasets. It is commonly used in market basket analysis to discover product associations (e.g., customers who buy bread often buy butter). Association rules have two key metrics: **support** (frequency of itemset occurrence) and **confidence** (likelihood of the rule being true). For example, {Milk} → {Cookies} with 80% confidence means that 80% of milk buyers also buy cookies. This technique helps businesses with cross-selling, inventory management, and marketing strategies.

119. What is the Apriori algorithm and where is it used?
Answer: The Apriori algorithm is a classic data mining algorithm used for mining frequent itemsets and discovering association rules. It uses a bottom-up approach where frequent subsets are extended one item at a time and groups that do not meet the minimum support are pruned. It is widely applied in retail for market basket analysis and also in bioinformatics and web usage mining. Despite being computationally intensive, Apriori is valued for its simplicity and effectiveness in generating interpretable rules. Optimizations and improvements like FP-Growth have been introduced to enhance its performance.

120. What is clustering in data mining and how is it useful?
Answer: Clustering is an unsupervised learning technique in data mining that involves grouping a set of data points into clusters so that items in the same group are more similar to each other than to those in other groups. Unlike classification, clustering does not use predefined labels. It is useful in customer segmentation, anomaly detection, image recognition, and document categorization. For example, businesses use clustering to group customers based on purchasing behavior to tailor marketing strategies. Common clustering algorithms include K-Means, DBSCAN, and Hierarchical Clustering.

121. What is the difference between classification and regression in data mining?
Answer: Classification and regression are both supervised learning techniques in data mining. Classification involves predicting discrete labels or categories (e.g., spam or not spam), while regression predicts continuous numerical values (e.g., house prices). Classification uses algorithms like Decision Trees, Naive Bayes, and Support Vector Machines, while regression models include Linear Regression and Regression Trees. The choice between them depends on the output variable. Classification helps in decision-making and fraud detection, whereas regression supports forecasting and trend analysis.

122. What is the curse of dimensionality in data mining?
Answer: The curse of dimensionality refers to various challenges that arise when analyzing data with a high number of features or dimensions. As the number of dimensions increases, the volume of the space increases exponentially, making the data sparse and reducing the effectiveness of traditional distance-based algorithms. It leads to issues like overfitting, increased computation time, and difficulty in visualizing data. Dimensionality reduction techniques such as Principal Component Analysis (PCA) or feature selection are used to mitigate this problem, improving performance and model accuracy.

123. What is data preprocessing and why is it important in data mining?
Answer: Data preprocessing is a critical step in data mining that involves cleaning, transforming, and preparing raw data for analysis. It includes tasks such as handling missing values, removing duplicates, normalization, encoding categorical variables, and outlier detection. Preprocessing ensures data quality and integrity, which directly impacts the accuracy of mining results. Poor data quality can lead to misleading patterns or models. Properly preprocessed data enhances model training, reduces noise, and improves the reliability of analytical outcomes.

124. What is the difference between supervised and unsupervised learning?
Answer: Supervised learning uses labeled data to train models that can predict outcomes or classify inputs (e.g., predicting exam scores or email spam detection). It includes classification and regression techniques. Unsupervised learning, by contrast, deals with unlabeled data to find hidden patterns or structures, such as clustering or association rule mining. Supervised learning needs a target variable, while unsupervised learning works with input variables only. Supervised learning is used in forecasting and diagnostics, whereas unsupervised learning is used in segmentation, recommendation systems, and anomaly detection.

125. What are some real-world applications of data warehousing and data mining?
Answer: Data warehousing and data mining have numerous applications across industries. In retail, they help in customer behavior analysis and inventory optimization. In finance, they support fraud detection, credit scoring, and risk management. Healthcare uses them for patient data analysis, disease prediction, and drug discovery. Telecommunication companies utilize them for churn analysis and service optimization. Education institutions apply them to student performance tracking and curriculum design. These technologies empower organizations to derive actionable insights, enhance operational efficiency, and gain a competitive advantage through data-driven decision-making.

121. What is denormalization in data warehousing?
Answer: Denormalization is the process of combining tables or adding redundant data in a relational database to improve read performance, particularly in data warehousing. Unlike normalization, which reduces redundancy for data integrity, denormalization simplifies query logic by reducing joins. For example, a single dimension table may include all attributes of a product instead of splitting them into related tables. Denormalization enhances query speed in star schemas and is well-suited for read-heavy environments like OLAP systems.

122. What is query rewriting in data warehouses?
Answer: Query rewriting is an optimization technique in which incoming queries are modified or restructured for improved performance without changing their results. It may involve replacing complex joins with simpler expressions, using materialized views, or applying indexing strategies. Query rewriting is performed by the query optimizer and helps in reducing execution time, especially in large data warehouses. It allows transparent optimization where users don't have to alter their queries to benefit from performance improvements.

123. What are conformed dimensions?
Answer: Conformed dimensions are dimension tables that are shared across multiple fact tables or data marts within

a data warehouse. They provide a consistent view of business entities, such as time, customer, or geography, ensuring uniformity in analysis and reporting. Conformed dimensions enable integration across different business areas and support enterprise-wide analytics. By standardizing attributes and hierarchies, they facilitate accurate comparisons, reduce redundancy, and improve data quality throughout the data warehousing ecosystem.

124. What is the difference between fact tables and dimension tables?
Answer: Fact tables contain measurable quantitative data (facts) such as sales, revenue, or profit, while dimension tables store descriptive attributes related to those facts, like product names, dates, or locations. Fact tables are typically large and normalized, holding foreign keys to associated dimension tables. Dimension tables are denormalized for easy navigation and analysis. The combination of these tables in star or snowflake schemas supports multidimensional analysis in data warehousing. Understanding this distinction is fundamental to designing effective warehouse schemas.

125. What is the use of ETL staging area?
Answer: The ETL staging area is a temporary storage location where raw data is placed before it is transformed and loaded into the data warehouse. It acts as an intermediate buffer between data sources and the warehouse, allowing for data cleansing, validation, deduplication, and auditing. The staging area helps isolate processing, reduces risk of corrupting warehouse data, and improves performance by offloading heavy transformations. It is a critical component in the ETL architecture, ensuring data quality and process reliability.

Chapter 7: Most Asked Questions Part-B

1. What is OLAP and how is it used in data warehousing?
Answer: Online Analytical Processing (OLAP) is a category of software tools that provides analysis of data stored in a data warehouse. OLAP allows users to interactively analyze multidimensional data from multiple perspectives, which supports decision-making processes. It helps in summarizing, consolidating, viewing, and analyzing data based on various dimensions such as time, geography, and products. OLAP operations include roll-up, drill-down, slice, and dice, which enable users to explore data at different levels of granularity. OLAP systems are categorized into MOLAP (Multidimensional OLAP), ROLAP (Relational OLAP), and HOLAP (Hybrid OLAP), depending on how data is stored and accessed. These tools are crucial in transforming raw data into meaningful insights for business intelligence.

2. What are the key characteristics of data mining?
Answer: Data mining involves discovering patterns, correlations, trends, or useful information from large sets of data using statistical, mathematical, and machine learning techniques. Key characteristics of data mining include the ability to handle large datasets, automatic pattern discovery, scalability, prediction of future trends, and integration with various data sources. It involves processes like classification, clustering, association rule mining, and regression. Data mining can be applied across domains such as marketing, finance, healthcare, and e-commerce to derive valuable insights and support decision-making. Its main goal is to extract knowledge that is understandable, novel, valid, and actionable.

3. How does data warehousing differ from a traditional database system?
Answer: Data warehousing differs from traditional database systems in terms of purpose, structure, and usage. While traditional databases are optimized for transaction processing (OLTP), data warehouses are optimized for analytical processing (OLAP). Data warehouses store historical data and are designed to support complex queries, trend analysis, and decision support. They use denormalized schemas like star and snowflake to facilitate faster querying, whereas traditional databases often use normalized schemas to reduce redundancy. Additionally, data warehouses consolidate data from multiple sources, clean and transform it, and organize it for business analysis, unlike traditional databases which handle day-to-day operational data.

4. What is a snowflake schema and how is it different from a star schema?
Answer: A snowflake schema is a type of multidimensional database schema that is a more normalized version of the star schema. In a snowflake schema, dimension tables are broken down into sub-dimension tables to eliminate redundancy. This leads to more complex joins but reduces data storage requirements. For example, a "Location" dimension might be normalized into separate tables for country, state, and city. In contrast, a star schema uses a single large denormalized dimension table directly linked to the fact table. While the star schema offers better performance due to simpler joins, the snowflake schema provides a more structured and organized model with reduced redundancy.

5. What are fact and dimension tables in data warehousing?
Answer: Fact and dimension tables are core components of a data warehouse schema. A fact table contains quantitative data for analysis and typically includes metrics, measurements, or facts of a business process (e.g., sales, revenue). It is surrounded by dimension tables, which provide the context for the facts, such as time, location, customer, or product. The fact table uses foreign keys to link to primary keys in the dimension tables. This structure forms a star or snowflake schema. While the fact table holds the data to be analyzed, dimension tables allow slicing and dicing the data in different ways, making it easier for users to perform meaningful analysis.

6. What is the ETL process in data warehousing?
Answer: ETL stands for Extract, Transform, and Load, which are the three main stages of data movement in a data warehousing system. Extraction involves retrieving data from various source systems like databases, flat files, or web services. Transformation applies business rules to convert the extracted data into a suitable format, including tasks like data cleansing, aggregation, and formatting. Finally, loading involves writing the transformed data into the data warehouse. ETL processes ensure data consistency, accuracy, and reliability, which are critical for meaningful data analysis. Automated ETL tools like Informatica, Talend, and Apache NiFi help streamline this process efficiently.

7. What are the advantages of using data mining in business applications?
Answer: Data mining provides numerous advantages in business applications by enabling organizations to uncover

hidden patterns and make data-driven decisions. It enhances customer relationship management through segmentation and behavior prediction. It helps in detecting fraud, improving product recommendations, managing risk, and optimizing operations. Businesses can also use data mining to forecast trends, increase revenue, and reduce costs. For instance, retailers can analyze purchasing patterns to optimize inventory and layout. Overall, data mining transforms raw data into actionable insights, giving businesses a competitive edge by improving strategic and operational decisions.

8. What is association rule mining?
Answer: Association rule mining is a data mining technique used to discover interesting relationships, patterns, or associations between variables in large datasets. It is commonly used in market basket analysis to identify products frequently bought together. The key metrics used in association rule mining are support, confidence, and lift. Support indicates how frequently the itemset appears in the dataset, confidence shows the likelihood of the consequent given the antecedent, and lift measures how much more often the rule occurs than expected. Algorithms like Apriori and FP-Growth are used for generating association rules. This technique helps businesses with cross-selling strategies and customer behavior analysis.

9. What is a data mart and how does it differ from a data warehouse?
Answer: A data mart is a subset of a data warehouse that focuses on a specific business area or department, such as sales, finance, or marketing. It contains data relevant to a particular group of users and is designed for their specific analytical needs. In contrast, a data warehouse is a centralized repository that integrates data from across the organization. Data marts can be created in two ways: top-down (derived from a central warehouse) or bottom-up (built first and integrated later into a warehouse). Data marts allow quicker access to data, faster query performance, and simplified data models for specific business users.

10. What is the role of metadata in data warehousing?
Answer: Metadata in data warehousing provides information about the data—essentially data about data. It describes the structure, source, transformation rules, and lineage of the data stored in the warehouse. Metadata helps users understand where the data came from, how it was processed, and how to interpret it correctly. There are two main types: technical metadata (used by IT professionals to manage data) and business metadata (used by end-users for understanding data meaning). Metadata improves data governance, enhances data quality, and supports efficient querying and reporting. It also aids in impact analysis and change management within data warehousing systems.

11. What is clustering in data mining?
Answer: Clustering is a data mining technique used to group similar data points together based on certain characteristics. Unlike classification, clustering is an unsupervised learning method, meaning it does not rely on predefined class labels. Each group or "cluster" contains data items that are more similar to each other than to those in other clusters. Common clustering algorithms include K-means, DBSCAN, and hierarchical clustering. Clustering is widely used in customer segmentation, image recognition, pattern detection, and market research. It helps analysts discover natural groupings in data and derive meaningful insights without prior knowledge of the data structure.

12. What is dimensionality reduction and why is it important in data mining?
Answer: Dimensionality reduction is the process of reducing the number of input variables in a dataset. It helps simplify models, reduce computation time, and eliminate redundant or irrelevant features. This process is crucial in data mining as high-dimensional data can be difficult to visualize and may lead to overfitting. Techniques like Principal Component Analysis (PCA), t-SNE, and Linear Discriminant Analysis (LDA) are commonly used. By focusing on the most informative features, dimensionality reduction improves the efficiency and performance of data mining models while maintaining the integrity of the data patterns.

13. How is anomaly detection used in data mining?
Answer: Anomaly detection, also known as outlier detection, is a technique used to identify rare or unusual patterns in data that do not conform to expected behavior. It is crucial in applications like fraud detection, network intrusion detection, and fault diagnosis. Anomalies can indicate critical incidents, such as fraudulent transactions or system failures. Methods for anomaly detection include statistical techniques, clustering-based approaches, and machine learning algorithms. The goal is to improve the reliability and security of systems by flagging potentially harmful or unexpected events based on historical data patterns.

14. What is the role of a data warehouse administrator?
Answer: A data warehouse administrator is responsible for the setup, maintenance, and performance of the data warehouse system. Their duties include data integration, ETL process monitoring, schema management, security enforcement, and ensuring high availability and data consistency. They collaborate with database administrators, developers, and business analysts to optimize queries, manage storage, and ensure the warehouse meets user needs. They also handle upgrades, backups, and recovery processes. The administrator plays a key role in maintaining data integrity and supporting data-driven decision-making across the organization.

15. What is the difference between classification and regression in data mining?
Answer: Classification and regression are both supervised learning techniques in data mining, but they serve different purposes. Classification is used when the output variable is categorical, such as classifying emails as spam or not spam. Regression, on the other hand, is used for predicting continuous numerical values, such as forecasting sales or predicting house prices. Classification algorithms include Decision Trees, Naive Bayes, and Support Vector Machines, while regression algorithms include Linear Regression and Random Forest Regressor. Both techniques help organizations make informed decisions, but their choice depends on the nature of the data and the problem at hand.

16. How does K-means clustering work?
Answer: K-means clustering is a popular algorithm used to partition data into K distinct clusters. The algorithm starts by randomly selecting K centroids, which represent the center of each cluster. Each data point is assigned to the nearest centroid based on Euclidean distance. Then, the centroids are recalculated by computing the mean of all data points in each cluster. This process is repeated iteratively until the centroids no longer change significantly, indicating convergence. K-means is efficient for large datasets but sensitive to the initial choice of centroids and the value of K. It works well when clusters are spherical and evenly sized.

17. What are surrogate keys and why are they used in data warehousing?
Answer: Surrogate keys are artificially generated unique identifiers used as primary keys in dimension tables in a data warehouse. Unlike natural keys, which originate from operational systems (like employee ID or product code), surrogate keys are typically sequential numbers generated during the ETL process. They provide several advantages: ensuring consistency when natural keys change, supporting slowly changing dimensions, and improving join performance. Surrogate keys help maintain historical data integrity and decouple the warehouse schema from changes in source systems, thus enhancing flexibility and reliability.

18. What is data preprocessing in data mining?
Answer: Data preprocessing is a crucial step in the data mining process that involves cleaning and transforming raw data into a suitable format for analysis. It includes data cleaning (handling missing values and removing noise), data integration (combining data from multiple sources), data transformation (normalization and encoding), and data reduction (feature selection and dimensionality reduction). Proper preprocessing ensures that data mining algorithms produce accurate and meaningful results. Without it, models may be misled by inconsistent, incomplete, or irrelevant data, leading to poor predictions or misleading insights.

19. What is the difference between supervised and unsupervised learning in data mining?
Answer: Supervised learning uses labeled data to train algorithms, allowing them to predict outcomes for new, unseen data. It is commonly used in classification and regression tasks where input-output pairs are known. Unsupervised learning, on the other hand, deals with unlabeled data and aims to discover hidden patterns or groupings within the dataset, such as clustering or association rule mining. While supervised learning requires prior knowledge about the data labels, unsupervised learning is exploratory and helps understand the data structure. Both approaches are integral to different stages of data mining and business intelligence.

20. What is data transformation and what are its types in the ETL process?
Answer: Data transformation is the process of converting data from its source format into a suitable format for analysis and storage in a data warehouse. This step occurs during the ETL process and includes operations like data cleansing, aggregation, encoding, and normalization. Common types of data transformation include format conversion (e.g., date formats), scaling (e.g., min-max normalization), deriving new values (e.g., total revenue = quantity × price), and joining multiple sources. Effective data transformation ensures that data is standardized, accurate, and ready for meaningful analysis in the warehouse environment.

21. What are the challenges of data warehousing?
Answer: Data warehousing presents several challenges, including data integration from heterogeneous sources, maintaining data quality, managing large volumes of data, and ensuring timely data updates. Designing an effective schema that supports both performance and scalability can be complex. Other challenges include dealing with slowly changing dimensions, security concerns, and high implementation and maintenance costs. Furthermore, aligning the data warehouse with business goals and user expectations requires ongoing communication and collaboration between IT and business teams. Overcoming these challenges is essential for delivering reliable and actionable insights.

22. How does a decision tree algorithm work in classification tasks?
Answer: A decision tree algorithm uses a tree-like structure to classify data by splitting it into branches based on feature values. Each internal node represents a decision on an attribute, each branch corresponds to an outcome of the decision, and each leaf node represents a class label or decision. The algorithm selects the feature that provides the highest information gain or lowest Gini impurity at each step. It continues to split the dataset recursively until it reaches a stopping criterion, such as a minimum node size or maximum depth. Decision trees are easy to interpret and work well for both classification and regression tasks.

23. What is data cleaning and why is it important in data mining?
Answer: Data cleaning is the process of identifying and correcting errors, inconsistencies, and inaccuracies in data before analysis. It involves handling missing values, removing duplicates, correcting formatting issues, and validating data integrity. Data cleaning is essential in data mining because poor-quality data can lead to misleading patterns, inaccurate predictions, and flawed decisions. Clean data ensures that data mining models are built on reliable inputs, improving the trustworthiness and value of the insights derived from the analysis.

24. What is the Apriori algorithm used for in data mining?
Answer: The Apriori algorithm is used for mining frequent itemsets and generating association rules from transactional databases. It operates on the principle that all non-empty subsets of a frequent itemset must also be frequent. The algorithm works in a level-wise manner: it begins with frequent single items, extends them to larger itemsets by joining them, and prunes those that do not meet a minimum support threshold. Apriori is commonly applied in market basket analysis to find items that are often bought together. It helps businesses optimize product placement, bundling, and promotional strategies.

25. What is a cube in OLAP and how is it used?
Answer: In OLAP, a cube is a multidimensional data structure that allows fast analysis of data according to different dimensions. Each axis of the cube represents a dimension (such as time, product, location), and the cells contain aggregated measures (such as sales or profit). OLAP cubes enable users to perform complex analytical queries, such as slicing (viewing a single layer of the cube), dicing (viewing a subcube), drilling down (increasing detail), and rolling up (summarizing data). OLAP cubes help in exploring data interactively and support decision-making by presenting data from multiple perspectives.

26. What is a snowflake schema in data warehousing?
Answer: A snowflake schema is a type of data warehouse schema that represents multidimensional data with normalized dimension tables. In this schema, dimension tables are split into additional tables to reduce redundancy and improve data integrity. For example, a "Location" dimension might be divided into "Country", "State", and "City" tables. Although it consumes less disk space and supports easier updates, querying in a snowflake schema can be slower due to the increased number of joins. It is more complex than a star schema but is preferred when normalization and data consistency are top priorities.

27. What is association rule mining in data mining?
Answer: Association rule mining is a data mining technique used to identify interesting relationships, patterns, or associations among items in large datasets. It is commonly used in market basket analysis to discover products that are frequently purchased together. For example, the rule {bread} → {butter} means that customers who buy bread often also buy butter. Two important metrics in association rule mining are support (how frequently the items appear together) and confidence (how often the rule holds true). Algorithms like Apriori and FP-Growth are widely used to extract these rules from transactional databases.

28. How do slowly changing dimensions (SCD) affect data warehousing?
Answer: Slowly changing dimensions (SCD) refer to attributes in dimension tables that change over time, such as a customer's address or marital status. Handling SCDs is important for maintaining historical accuracy in data warehouses. There are several types: Type 1 overwrites old data, Type 2 creates a new record to preserve history, and Type 3 stores the previous value in a separate column. Choosing the right approach depends on the business need—whether history should be retained or overwritten. Proper SCD management ensures accurate time-based analysis and reporting.

29. What is the role of metadata in a data warehouse?
Answer: Metadata in a data warehouse provides information about the structure, operations, and content of the warehouse. It acts as a roadmap for users and tools to understand how data is organized and managed. Metadata is classified into technical metadata (e.g., table definitions, data types), business metadata (e.g., definitions of KPIs), and operational metadata (e.g., data load schedules). It helps with data governance, lineage tracking, and simplifies the ETL process. Metadata is essential for effective warehouse administration, documentation, and for enabling self-service business intelligence.

30. What is the role of a data mart in data warehousing?
Answer: A data mart is a smaller, more focused version of a data warehouse designed to serve the specific needs of a department or business unit. It contains a subset of data relevant to a particular function, such as sales, marketing, or finance. Data marts improve performance by limiting the data scope and reduce complexity for end-users. They can be dependent (sourced from the central warehouse) or independent (sourced directly from operational systems). Data marts enable faster querying and analysis while supporting the broader goals of enterprise data warehousing.

31. What is the importance of normalization in a data warehouse?
Answer: Normalization in a data warehouse involves organizing data to reduce redundancy and improve data integrity. It is typically applied to dimension tables in a snowflake schema. While normalization results in more tables and complex joins, it ensures consistency and simplifies updates. However, excessive normalization can impact query performance. Therefore, a balanced approach is used in data warehousing: dimension tables may be partially normalized while fact tables are usually denormalized for faster querying. Proper normalization contributes to a well-structured and maintainable warehouse environment.

32. What is the difference between OLTP and OLAP?
Answer: OLTP (Online Transaction Processing) and OLAP (Online Analytical Processing) are two different types of data systems. OLTP systems manage day-to-day transactions such as order entry and banking, focusing on speed and data integrity. OLAP systems, on the other hand, are designed for analytical purposes, enabling users to perform complex queries and generate reports. OLTP uses normalized schemas, whereas OLAP typically uses star or snowflake schemas. OLTP deals with real-time operations, while OLAP supports decision-making based on historical data analysis.

33. What is data discretization in data mining?
Answer: Data discretization is the process of converting continuous data into discrete buckets or intervals. It simplifies data, reduces model complexity, and is essential for algorithms that require categorical input. Discretization can be supervised (using class labels) or unsupervised (based solely on data distribution). Techniques include equal-width binning, equal-frequency binning, and clustering-based discretization. It is commonly used in decision tree learning and rule-based classifiers, enhancing interpretability and performance in data mining tasks.

34. What is an ETL pipeline?
Answer: An ETL pipeline refers to the sequence of processes involved in extracting data from source systems, transforming it into a suitable format, and loading it into a data warehouse. The pipeline handles data cleaning, validation, integration, and aggregation. Modern ETL pipelines may also include real-time processing and data quality monitoring. A well-designed ETL pipeline ensures timely and accurate data delivery, supports business intelligence activities, and forms the backbone of the data warehousing architecture.

35. What is the use of the FP-Growth algorithm in data mining?
Answer: The FP-Growth (Frequent Pattern Growth) algorithm is used for mining frequent itemsets without candidate generation, which makes it faster and more scalable than Apriori. It compresses the dataset into a compact structure

called an FP-tree and extracts frequent patterns using recursive methods. FP-Growth significantly reduces the time complexity for large datasets and is especially useful in market basket analysis and other association rule mining tasks. Its efficiency makes it suitable for applications involving large volumes of transactional data.

36. What is data cube aggregation in OLAP?
Answer: Data cube aggregation refers to the process of summarizing data across multiple dimensions to support faster and more flexible OLAP queries. Aggregates are precomputed totals or averages for combinations of dimension levels, such as sales by region or time. This reduces query response time since computations are already available. Aggregation plays a critical role in roll-up operations, which involve moving from detailed to summary data. It enhances performance and enables multidimensional data analysis for strategic decision-making.

37. What is concept hierarchy in data warehousing?
Answer: A concept hierarchy defines a sequence of mappings from a set of low-level concepts to higher-level concepts. For example, in a location dimension, the hierarchy might be City → State → Country. Hierarchies enable OLAP operations like roll-up and drill-down by organizing data into multiple levels of abstraction. They enhance the usability of data cubes and improve analytical capabilities by allowing users to analyze data at various levels of granularity. Concept hierarchies also support summarization and trend analysis in business intelligence.

38. What are the components of a star schema?
Answer: A star schema consists of a central fact table connected to multiple dimension tables. The fact table contains quantitative data (e.g., sales, revenue) and foreign keys that link to the dimension tables. Each dimension table holds descriptive attributes (e.g., product name, customer location) related to the facts. The star schema is easy to understand and provides fast query performance due to fewer joins. It is widely used in data warehousing and OLAP applications for its simplicity and efficiency.

39. What is pruning in decision trees?
Answer: Pruning is a technique used to reduce the size of a decision tree by removing branches that do not contribute significantly to its predictive accuracy. It helps prevent overfitting by simplifying the model and improving generalization to unseen data. There are two types of pruning: pre-pruning (stopping tree growth early based on criteria like minimum samples) and post-pruning (removing branches after the tree is fully grown). Pruning results in more compact, interpretable, and robust models in classification tasks.

40. What is schema evolution in data warehousing?
Answer: Schema evolution refers to the ability of a data warehouse to adapt to changes in the data model over time. These changes may include adding new attributes, modifying existing ones, or redefining relationships. Schema evolution is necessary to accommodate business changes and maintain the relevance of the warehouse. It should be handled carefully to preserve historical data and ensure backward compatibility. Tools and techniques such as versioning, metadata tracking, and data migration support schema evolution while minimizing disruption to analytics processes.

41. What is the difference between supervised and unsupervised learning in data mining?
Answer: Supervised learning involves training a model on labeled data, where the outcome variable is known. It is used for tasks like classification and regression. In contrast, unsupervised learning works with unlabeled data to uncover hidden patterns or groupings, such as clustering or dimensionality reduction. Supervised learning evaluates the relationship between input and output, while unsupervised learning seeks inherent structures in the data. Both are essential in data mining for extracting meaningful insights depending on the availability of labeled data.

42. What is the role of a data staging area in a data warehouse?
Answer: A data staging area is a temporary storage location used during the ETL process in data warehousing. It holds raw data extracted from various source systems before transformation and loading into the data warehouse. The staging area supports data cleansing, transformation, de-duplication, and integration. It improves performance and data quality by isolating complex operations from the main warehouse and ensures consistency in the final loaded data. It is an essential component for reliable data management in warehouse environments

43. What is the purpose of surrogate keys in dimension tables?
Answer: Surrogate keys are artificial, unique identifiers used in dimension tables instead of natural keys from source

systems. They simplify joins between fact and dimension tables and ensure consistency even when the natural key changes. Surrogate keys prevent data anomalies caused by business rule changes or inconsistencies in source systems. They also improve performance by using integer values for indexing. Surrogate keys are a best practice in dimensional modeling for maintaining historical accuracy and referential integrity.

44. What is anomaly detection in data mining?
Answer: Anomaly detection involves identifying rare or unusual data points that deviate significantly from the norm. These anomalies can indicate critical incidents such as fraud, equipment failure, or data entry errors. Techniques include statistical methods, clustering, and machine learning algorithms like Isolation Forest or Autoencoders. Anomaly detection plays a key role in domains like cybersecurity, healthcare, and finance. It enables proactive decision-making by highlighting unexpected behavior in large datasets.

45. How is clustering used in data mining?
Answer: Clustering is an unsupervised data mining technique used to group similar data points into clusters based on shared characteristics. It helps discover hidden patterns and structures in data without prior labels. Common clustering algorithms include K-Means, Hierarchical Clustering, and DBSCAN. Applications of clustering include customer segmentation, image analysis, and anomaly detection. By identifying natural groupings, clustering supports targeted marketing, personalized services, and efficient resource allocation.

46. What is the difference between classification and regression in data mining?
Answer: Classification and regression are both supervised learning techniques, but they serve different purposes. Classification predicts categorical outcomes (e.g., spam or not spam), while regression predicts continuous values (e.g., house prices). Classification models include decision trees, SVM, and Naive Bayes, whereas regression uses linear regression, ridge regression, and others. The choice between them depends on the type of output variable and the business objective. Both are fundamental in building predictive analytics solutions.

47. What is a dimensional model in data warehousing?
Answer: A dimensional model organizes data into fact and dimension tables to support analytical queries in a data warehouse. Fact tables contain measurable data, while dimension tables provide descriptive context. Dimensional modeling simplifies complex database structures, enabling faster queries and better understanding for business users. Popular schemas include star and snowflake schemas. This model is the foundation for OLAP systems and is critical for effective business intelligence and reporting.

48. What is data mining in the context of business intelligence?
Answer: In business intelligence, data mining is the process of analyzing large datasets to discover patterns, trends, and relationships that inform strategic decisions. It uses statistical, machine learning, and database techniques to extract actionable insights. Data mining supports use cases such as customer segmentation, sales forecasting, and risk assessment. It complements reporting and visualization tools by providing deeper analysis, enabling organizations to gain a competitive edge through data-driven decisions.

49. What is role-based access control in a data warehouse?
Answer: Role-based access control (RBAC) restricts data access based on a user's role within the organization. In a data warehouse, RBAC ensures that users can only access data and perform actions relevant to their responsibilities. It improves data security, compliance, and governance by preventing unauthorized access. Roles are predefined with permissions, and users are assigned to roles accordingly. RBAC simplifies administration and aligns data access with organizational policies and hierarchy.

50. What is time-variant data in a data warehouse?
Answer: Time-variant data refers to the capability of a data warehouse to store and manage historical data over time. Unlike operational databases that focus on current transactions, a data warehouse tracks changes and trends by capturing time-based snapshots. Time variance allows for trend analysis, historical comparisons, and audits. It is implemented using effective dates, timestamps, or slowly changing dimensions. Supporting time-variant data is essential for comprehensive analytics and long-term business planning.

51. What is drill-down analysis in data mining?
Answer: Drill-down analysis is a data mining technique that allows users to view data at increasing levels of detail.

Starting from a broad overview, users can click or "drill down" to explore more granular levels of information. For example, from a yearly sales report, a user may drill down into quarterly, monthly, or even daily sales data. This helps uncover trends, outliers, or anomalies that are not visible at higher levels. Drill-down analysis is essential for business intelligence as it enhances data exploration, supports root-cause analysis, and provides deeper insights for decision-making.

52. How does OLAP support decision making in businesses?
Answer: OLAP (Online Analytical Processing) supports decision-making by enabling multidimensional analysis of large volumes of data. It allows users to perform operations like slicing, dicing, drilling, and pivoting across various dimensions such as time, geography, and product categories. OLAP helps businesses identify patterns, monitor performance, and evaluate trends over time. It offers fast, interactive responses that enhance user experience and enables managers to gain meaningful insights from historical and real-time data. This facilitates better forecasting, strategic planning, and quicker response to market changes.

53. What are surrogate keys and why are they used in data warehousing?
Answer: Surrogate keys are artificial or system-generated keys used in a data warehouse to uniquely identify records in dimension tables. Unlike natural keys, which are derived from business data (like customer IDs), surrogate keys are typically integers with no business meaning. They are used to avoid problems caused by changes in source data, ensure data integrity, and maintain consistency in relationships between tables. Surrogate keys simplify data warehouse design, support slowly changing dimensions (SCDs), and provide better performance in queries due to their numeric nature.

54. What is metadata in data warehousing?
Answer: Metadata is data about data in a data warehouse environment. It provides information about the structure, source, transformation, and usage of data. Metadata includes details such as table definitions, data types, ETL rules, column descriptions, and business rules. It acts as a guide for users and tools, helping them understand and manage data effectively. There are three types of metadata: technical, business, and operational. Accurate metadata management enhances data governance, promotes transparency, and supports efficient data warehousing operations and maintenance.

55. What is the role of a staging area in a data warehouse?
Answer: A staging area is an intermediate storage space where data from multiple sources is temporarily stored before it is transformed and loaded into the data warehouse. It plays a critical role in the ETL (Extract, Transform, Load) process by facilitating data cleansing, validation, integration, and transformation. The staging area allows for efficient handling of raw data, reducing the risk of corrupting warehouse data during preprocessing. It also helps manage load performance, data consistency, and error handling, ensuring high-quality, reliable data for analytics and reporting.

56. What are factless fact tables?
Answer: Factless fact tables are fact tables that do not contain any numeric or measurable facts but instead capture events or relationships. They are used to record the occurrence of specific events, such as student attendance, employee leaves, or product promotions. There are two types: event-tracking and coverage factless fact tables. These tables help in analyzing business activities, identifying gaps, and supporting many-to-many relationships. Though they lack traditional measures, they provide valuable insights when analyzed alongside dimension tables and are an important design element in dimensional modeling.

57. What is cube slicing in OLAP?
Answer: Cube slicing is an OLAP operation that involves selecting a single layer (slice) of a data cube by fixing one dimension to a specific value. This reduces the multidimensional cube into a two-dimensional view for easier analysis. For example, slicing a sales cube by selecting data for the year 2024 will show sales across products and regions for that specific year. Cube slicing enhances data exploration by narrowing the scope of analysis, supports focused decision-making, and simplifies visualization and reporting.

58. What are the key responsibilities of a data warehouse administrator (DWA)?
Answer: A data warehouse administrator is responsible for the management, maintenance, and optimization of the data warehouse environment. Key duties include monitoring data loads, managing metadata, tuning performance, securing access, handling backup and recovery, and ensuring data quality. The DWA coordinates with data engineers,

analysts, and business users to ensure smooth ETL operations and consistent data availability. They also manage storage resources, troubleshoot errors, and implement upgrades. Their role is critical in maintaining the efficiency, reliability, and scalability of the data warehousing system.

59. What are data cubes and how do they work?
Answer: Data cubes are multidimensional arrays of data used in OLAP systems to enable fast and efficient querying and analysis. Each cell in a data cube represents a measure (such as sales) along intersecting dimensions (like time, location, and product). Data cubes allow users to perform multidimensional analysis using operations like slicing, dicing, drilling, and pivoting. They support summarized and aggregated data, enabling quick insights and real-time decision-making. By precomputing and organizing data efficiently, data cubes significantly improve the performance of analytical queries.

60. What is the difference between operational databases and data warehouses?
Answer: Operational databases are designed for real-time transactional processing (OLTP), focusing on data accuracy, speed, and concurrency. They support day-to-day operations such as order entry, payroll, or customer management. Data warehouses, on the other hand, are optimized for analytical processing (OLAP), storing historical data from multiple sources for reporting and decision-making. While operational databases prioritize updates and transactions, data warehouses emphasize query performance, data integration, and long-term storage. These systems serve different purposes but work together to support comprehensive enterprise data management.

61. What is anomaly detection in data mining?
Answer: Anomaly detection is the process of identifying unusual patterns or behaviors in data that do not conform to expected norms. These anomalies could represent critical incidents such as fraud, network intrusions, or equipment failures. Techniques used for anomaly detection include statistical methods, clustering, classification, and neural networks. In data mining, anomaly detection helps in improving decision-making, ensuring data integrity, and identifying hidden issues that could affect operations. It plays a significant role in domains like cybersecurity, healthcare, finance, and manufacturing.

62. How is data quality maintained in data warehousing?
Answer: Data quality in data warehousing is maintained through several processes during the ETL cycle. These include data profiling, cleansing, standardization, validation, and transformation. Duplicate removal, handling missing values, correcting inconsistencies, and aligning formats ensure data is accurate and reliable. Implementing strong metadata management, audit trails, and data governance policies also strengthens data quality. High-quality data improves analytics, reporting, and business insights, leading to better decision-making across the organization.

63. What is a hybrid data warehouse architecture?
Answer: A hybrid data warehouse architecture combines traditional on-premises storage with cloud-based data storage and processing. This architecture leverages the advantages of both environments—security and control from on-premises systems and scalability and cost-effectiveness from cloud platforms. It enables organizations to manage large datasets efficiently, adopt real-time analytics, and support modern big data tools. The hybrid approach allows gradual cloud adoption, offers better disaster recovery, and supports diverse workloads and user needs across departments.

64. What is the importance of ETL testing in a data warehouse?
Answer: ETL testing is crucial to ensure that data is accurately extracted from source systems, transformed correctly according to business rules, and loaded into the data warehouse without loss or corruption. It verifies data integrity, consistency, and performance across the ETL process. ETL testing identifies errors early, prevents data quality issues, and ensures that reports and analytics are based on trustworthy data. It includes validation of data mappings, reconciliation of row counts, and testing of business logic and data transformations.

65. How are hierarchical dimensions handled in data warehousing?
Answer: Hierarchical dimensions are handled using parent-child or level-based structures in dimension tables. For example, a geography dimension might include levels like Country → State → City. These hierarchies support roll-up (aggregating data up the hierarchy) and drill-down operations in OLAP analysis. Dimensional modeling techniques like star or snowflake schemas are used to represent these hierarchies. Managing hierarchical dimensions enhances analytical capabilities and provides meaningful aggregations for business intelligence.

66. What is the use of a time dimension in a data warehouse?
Answer: The time dimension is a critical component in a data warehouse as it allows for the analysis of data over time. It includes attributes such as day, week, month, quarter, and year, along with flags for holidays, weekends, and fiscal periods. The time dimension enables users to perform trend analysis, seasonal analysis, and time-based comparisons. It supports operations like rolling averages, YTD (Year-to-Date) metrics, and time series forecasting, making it essential for business performance analysis.

67. What is dimensional modeling and why is it important?
Answer: Dimensional modeling is a data design technique used in data warehousing to optimize data retrieval for analytical queries. It organizes data into fact and dimension tables in a star or snowflake schema. This approach simplifies complex data structures, enhances query performance, and makes data more intuitive for users. Dimensional modeling supports consistent and scalable design, improves maintainability, and enables effective reporting and decision support systems by making it easier to analyze business metrics across different perspectives.

68. How does parallel processing improve data warehouse performance?
Answer: Parallel processing divides large data tasks into smaller chunks that can be processed simultaneously across multiple processors or nodes. In data warehousing, it is used to speed up ETL operations, complex queries, and data loading tasks. This approach reduces processing time, enhances scalability, and ensures timely availability of data for analytics. Technologies like Massively Parallel Processing (MPP) databases and distributed file systems leverage parallel processing to handle big data workloads efficiently and reliably.

69. What is the difference between normalized and denormalized data structures in warehousing?
Answer: Normalized data structures reduce data redundancy and improve data integrity by organizing data into multiple related tables. This is suitable for operational databases but may lead to complex queries in analytical systems. Denormalized structures, common in data warehousing, combine data into fewer tables to optimize read performance and simplify reporting. While normalization supports data consistency, denormalization supports query speed and ease of use in business intelligence environments, often using star or snowflake schemas.

70. What is a data mart and how does it differ from a data warehouse?
Answer: A data mart is a subset of a data warehouse focused on a specific business line or department, such as sales or finance. It contains a smaller volume of data and is tailored for the analytical needs of its users. A data warehouse, on the other hand, is an enterprise-wide repository that integrates data from multiple sources across the organization. Data marts are faster to implement, cost-effective, and easier to manage, while data warehouses provide a holistic view of the enterprise.

71. What is clustering in data mining?
Answer: Clustering is a data mining technique that groups similar data objects into clusters based on shared characteristics or patterns. Unlike classification, clustering is an unsupervised learning method that doesn't rely on labeled data. Common clustering algorithms include K-means, DBSCAN, and hierarchical clustering. Clustering is used in customer segmentation, market analysis, anomaly detection, and pattern recognition. It helps uncover hidden structures in data and supports data summarization, trend analysis, and decision-making.

72. What is confidence in association rule mining?
Answer: Confidence is a metric used in association rule mining to measure the likelihood that a rule will be true for a new dataset. It is calculated as the ratio of the number of transactions containing both items A and B to the number of transactions containing item A. In the rule $A \rightarrow B$, confidence measures how often B appears in transactions that also contain A. High confidence indicates strong association and reliability of the rule in predicting outcomes.

73. How does data integration impact data warehousing?
Answer: Data integration involves combining data from multiple heterogeneous sources into a unified view, which is essential in building a data warehouse. It ensures consistency, accuracy, and completeness by resolving conflicts, standardizing formats, and matching schemas. Effective data integration improves the quality of data available for analysis, enhances decision-making, and supports real-time data access. It plays a critical role in ETL processes, metadata management, and maintaining a single version of truth across the enterprise.

74. What is MapReduce and how is it used in data mining?
Answer: MapReduce is a programming model developed by Google for processing large datasets in parallel across a distributed cluster. It consists of two phases: the Map phase, which processes input data into key-value pairs, and the Reduce phase, which aggregates and summarizes the output. In data mining, MapReduce is used to execute tasks like counting frequencies, building models, and performing large-scale statistical analysis. It supports scalability, fault-tolerance, and efficient handling of big data through frameworks like Hadoop.

75. What is pattern evaluation in data mining?
Answer: Pattern evaluation is the process of identifying the most useful and interesting patterns discovered during data mining. It involves applying measures such as support, confidence, lift, and interest to rank patterns based on their relevance and usefulness. Pattern evaluation helps eliminate redundant or insignificant patterns, focusing on those that provide actionable insights. It ensures that only meaningful knowledge is extracted from the data, facilitating better decisions and more accurate predictions in various domains like retail, finance, and healthcare.

76. What is the importance of metadata in a data warehouse?
Answer: Metadata in a data warehouse provides information about the data stored within, including its source, structure, transformation rules, and usage. It acts as a roadmap, helping users understand how data is organized, accessed, and utilized. Metadata supports ETL processes by documenting source-to-target mappings and assists business users by offering descriptions and definitions of data elements. It plays a crucial role in data governance, lineage tracking, auditing, and ensuring consistency and accuracy across analytical systems.

77. How does OLAP differ from OLTP in data warehousing?
Answer: OLAP (Online Analytical Processing) is designed for complex queries, analysis, and decision support, while OLTP (Online Transaction Processing) handles routine transactional operations. OLAP systems focus on read-heavy operations, data summarization, and multi-dimensional views of data using star or snowflake schemas. OLTP systems, on the other hand, manage insert, update, and delete operations with normalized databases to maintain data integrity. The fundamental difference lies in their usage: OLTP for daily operations and OLAP for strategic analysis.

78. What is the role of data transformation in ETL?
Answer: Data transformation is a critical step in the ETL (Extract, Transform, Load) process where extracted data is converted into a suitable format for analysis. It includes operations such as data cleansing, type conversion, normalization, aggregation, and applying business rules. Transformation ensures consistency across different sources and aligns data with the target schema. Proper transformation improves data quality, supports better decision-making, and enables efficient querying and reporting in the data warehouse.

79. What are surrogate keys and why are they used?
Answer: Surrogate keys are artificially generated identifiers used in data warehouse dimension tables to uniquely identify each record. Unlike natural keys, which are derived from operational data, surrogate keys are system-generated (e.g., auto-increment integers). They simplify data integration by providing consistency, help manage slowly changing dimensions, and enhance performance during joins. Surrogate keys also prevent issues that arise from changes in business keys, supporting stable and maintainable warehouse design.

80. What is the difference between star and snowflake schema?
Answer: The star schema is a simple database design where a central fact table connects directly to dimension tables. Each dimension contains denormalized data, making queries faster and easier to understand. In contrast, the snowflake schema normalizes dimension tables by splitting them into multiple related tables. This reduces data redundancy but adds complexity to queries. While star schema offers performance and simplicity, snowflake schema ensures better data integrity and storage efficiency.

81. What is discretization in data mining?
Answer: Discretization is the process of converting continuous numerical data into categorical or interval-based data. This is often required for certain data mining algorithms that work better with categorical inputs. Techniques include equal-width binning, equal-frequency binning, and clustering-based discretization. Discretization helps in simplifying models, improving accuracy, and reducing computational complexity. It is commonly used in classification, decision trees, and association rule mining to improve interpretability and performance.

82. What is the use of data profiling in a data warehouse?
Answer: Data profiling involves analyzing data sources to understand their structure, content, and quality before loading them into the data warehouse. It helps identify anomalies, inconsistencies, missing values, and patterns in the data. Profiling supports the design of data validation rules, improves data quality, and guides transformation logic in the ETL process. It also ensures that the data warehouse receives clean, structured, and reliable data for accurate analysis and reporting.

83. What is the difference between batch processing and stream processing?
Answer: Batch processing handles large volumes of data in groups or batches at scheduled intervals, making it ideal for complex computations that do not require real-time analysis. Stream processing, on the other hand, deals with continuous, real-time data flows, enabling instant analytics and responses. Batch processing is common in traditional ETL, while stream processing is used in applications like fraud detection and IoT analytics. Both approaches serve different purposes in a data architecture.

84. What is a cube in OLAP systems?
Answer: A cube in OLAP (Online Analytical Processing) systems is a multi-dimensional data structure that allows users to analyze data from different perspectives. Each dimension represents a distinct category, such as time, geography, or product. Cubes support operations like slicing, dicing, drilling, and pivoting, enabling interactive and in-depth data exploration. OLAP cubes are optimized for high-speed querying and aggregations, facilitating fast and flexible business intelligence analysis.

85. What are decision trees in data mining?
Answer: Decision trees are predictive models used in data mining for classification and regression tasks. They consist of nodes representing decisions based on attribute values, branches representing outcomes, and leaves indicating final results. Algorithms like ID3, C4.5, and CART are used to construct decision trees. These models are easy to interpret, handle both numerical and categorical data, and are effective for uncovering hidden patterns in large datasets. They are widely used in marketing, healthcare, and finance.

86. What is web mining and how is it categorized?
Answer: Web mining is the process of discovering patterns and useful information from web data, including content, structure, and usage data. It is categorized into three types: web content mining (analyzing web page content), web structure mining (analyzing link structures), and web usage mining (analyzing user behavior and access logs). Web mining helps in improving website design, personalization, recommendation systems, and market analysis by extracting insights from the vast amount of web data.

87. How do KPIs relate to data warehousing?
Answer: KPIs (Key Performance Indicators) are measurable values that indicate how effectively a business is achieving its objectives. In data warehousing, KPIs are derived from aggregated and historical data stored in fact tables. They are used in dashboards and reports to monitor business performance across various departments. By centralizing and standardizing KPI definitions, a data warehouse ensures consistent performance measurement and supports data-driven decision-making.

88. What is data governance and its role in data warehousing?
Answer: Data governance is a set of policies, procedures, and standards that ensure the effective management, quality, and security of data across the organization. In data warehousing, it helps maintain data integrity, compliance, and accountability. Data governance defines data ownership, access controls, metadata standards, and quality benchmarks. It plays a vital role in building trust in data, ensuring consistency, and supporting regulatory compliance such as GDPR or HIPAA.

89. What is a conformed dimension?
Answer: A conformed dimension is a dimension that is shared across multiple fact tables or data marts within a data warehouse. It ensures consistency and integration across different business areas by using the same dimension definitions, attributes, and hierarchies. For example, a "Customer" dimension used in both sales and service fact tables is conformed. Conformed dimensions support enterprise-wide analysis and promote reusability and standardization in dimensional modeling.

90. What are association rules in data mining?
Answer: Association rules are used in data mining to discover interesting relationships between variables in large datasets. They take the form of "If-Then" statements, such as "If a customer buys bread, they are likely to buy butter." These rules are evaluated using metrics like support, confidence, and lift. Association rule mining is widely applied in market basket analysis, recommendation systems, and customer behavior analysis to find hidden patterns and correlations.

91. What is scalability in data warehousing?
Answer: Scalability refers to the ability of a data warehouse to handle increasing volumes of data, users, and query loads without compromising performance. A scalable data warehouse can grow vertically (adding more resources to a server) or horizontally (adding more servers). It ensures consistent query performance, fast data loading, and minimal downtime as the organization grows. Scalability is achieved through optimized database design, indexing, partitioning, and the use of modern distributed technologies.

92. What are slowly changing dimensions (SCDs)?
Answer: Slowly changing dimensions are dimensions in a data warehouse that change over time, but not frequently. Managing SCDs is important to maintain historical accuracy and track changes in attributes. There are several types: Type 1 overwrites old data, Type 2 keeps history by adding new rows, and Type 3 keeps partial history using additional columns. Choosing the right method ensures data reflects either the current state or historical trends as needed for analysis.

93. How does data warehousing support business intelligence?
Answer: Data warehousing supports business intelligence by providing a centralized, integrated, and historical repository of data for reporting and analysis. It consolidates data from multiple sources, ensuring data quality and consistency. BI tools access the warehouse to generate dashboards, reports, and visualizations that help decision-makers monitor KPIs, identify trends, and forecast future outcomes. This support enables organizations to make informed, strategic decisions based on accurate and comprehensive data.

94. What is lift in association rule mining?
Answer: Lift is a measure used in association rule mining to evaluate the strength of a rule beyond random chance. It is calculated as the ratio of the observed support for items A and B occurring together to the expected support if A and B were independent. A lift value greater than 1 indicates a positive association between the items, suggesting that the occurrence of one item increases the likelihood of the other. Lift helps prioritize the most meaningful and actionable rules.

95. What is data granularity in a data warehouse?
Answer: Data granularity refers to the level of detail or summarization of data stored in the warehouse. High granularity means detailed data, such as individual transactions, while low granularity means aggregated data, such as daily or monthly summaries. The choice of granularity affects storage requirements, query performance, and the scope of analysis. Granular data allows more flexible and in-depth analysis, while summarized data supports faster queries and higher-level insights.

96. What are the key challenges in implementing a data warehouse?
Answer: Implementing a data warehouse involves several challenges, including data integration from various sources, maintaining data quality, and dealing with large data volumes. Complex ETL processes can lead to performance bottlenecks and inconsistencies. Ensuring consistency between real-time and historical data, adapting to frequent schema changes, and providing timely updates are other major hurdles. Moreover, high implementation costs, user training, and resistance to change can affect success. Security, governance, and compliance also play a critical role. Addressing these challenges requires robust planning, experienced teams, proper tools, and continuous monitoring to ensure a scalable and efficient data warehouse system.

97. What is surrogate key in data warehousing?
Answer: A surrogate key is an artificial or system-generated identifier used in a data warehouse to uniquely identify a record, especially in dimension tables. Unlike natural keys, surrogate keys have no business meaning and are typically sequential integers. They are used to simplify joins, improve performance, and maintain consistency across multiple systems. Surrogate keys help manage slowly changing dimensions (SCDs) by allowing multiple records for

the same natural key with different versioning. This technique also avoids changes in the fact tables when the business key of a dimension changes. Surrogate keys promote flexibility and data integrity in data warehousing.

98. What are slowly changing dimensions (SCDs)?
Answer: Slowly Changing Dimensions (SCDs) refer to dimensions in a data warehouse that change slowly over time rather than frequently. Managing such changes is critical for preserving historical accuracy and tracking evolution. There are several SCD types: Type 1 overwrites old data with new, Type 2 keeps historical data by adding new rows, and Type 3 adds new columns for limited history tracking. Selecting the correct SCD type depends on business requirements. Implementing SCDs involves careful design, versioning, and ETL strategies. Proper handling ensures accurate reporting and meaningful historical analysis.

99. What is data transformation in ETL?
Answer: Data transformation in ETL refers to the process of converting data from its source format into a format suitable for analysis in the target data warehouse. This step occurs after extraction and before loading. Transformation includes tasks such as data cleansing, aggregation, normalization, denormalization, encoding, and deriving calculated fields. It ensures consistency, accuracy, and compatibility across diverse data sources. Effective transformation improves data quality and enables better decision-making. Tools like Informatica, Talend, and SQL scripts are commonly used for transformation. This stage is critical to meet business logic, reporting requirements, and regulatory standards in the data warehouse.

100. What is metadata in data warehousing?
Answer: Metadata in data warehousing is data about data. It describes the structure, source, meaning, and usage of data stored in the warehouse. Metadata can be categorized into technical metadata (schemas, tables, columns, data types), business metadata (definitions, rules, KPIs), and operational metadata (ETL job logs, load times). It helps users understand and trust the data, facilitates efficient data discovery, and supports data governance. Metadata management tools enable documentation, impact analysis, lineage tracking, and quality control. A well-managed metadata repository improves transparency, accelerates development, and ensures consistency in reporting and analytics.

101. What is real-time data warehousing?
Answer: Real-time data warehousing refers to the process of capturing, transforming, and loading data into a warehouse system as soon as it is generated, enabling immediate analysis and decision-making. Unlike traditional batch-based warehousing, real-time systems support continuous data updates and provide the most current information. It is useful in applications such as fraud detection, inventory management, and online customer engagement. Implementing real-time data warehousing requires powerful ETL tools, in-memory processing, and support for streaming data platforms like Apache Kafka. It enhances responsiveness, reduces latency, and allows for more dynamic business intelligence.

102. What is the role of business intelligence in data warehousing?
Answer: Business Intelligence (BI) tools and processes play a crucial role in data warehousing by transforming raw data into actionable insights. BI utilizes data warehousing as a centralized source to perform analytics, generate reports, dashboards, and support strategic decision-making. It includes data visualization, ad-hoc querying, OLAP analysis, and predictive modeling. By leveraging data warehouses, BI ensures data consistency, historical accuracy, and cross-functional analysis. This integration empowers organizations to identify trends, optimize operations, and gain a competitive edge, making data warehousing the backbone of BI infrastructure.

103. What is a snowflake schema?
Answer: A snowflake schema is a type of database schema used in data warehousing that normalizes dimension tables into multiple related tables. Unlike a star schema where dimension tables are denormalized, snowflake schema structures allow dimensions to be broken down into sub-dimensions. For example, a "Location" dimension might be split into Country → State → City tables. Snowflake schemas reduce redundancy, improve data integrity, and save storage, but they may result in more complex queries and slower performance. They are best suited for environments where data normalization and detailed hierarchical relationships are important.

104. What is data profiling in data warehousing?
Answer: Data profiling is the process of examining source data to understand its structure, content, quality, and consistency before integrating it into a data warehouse. It helps identify anomalies, missing values, duplicates, data

types, and relationships. Profiling aids in designing accurate ETL processes, improving data quality, and validating business rules. It is typically done during the data preparation phase and is supported by tools like Talend, Informatica, and IBM InfoSphere. Effective data profiling ensures clean and reliable data, which is critical for the success of data warehousing and analytics projects.

105. What is data stewardship?
Answer: Data stewardship refers to the management and oversight of an organization's data assets to ensure high data quality, compliance, and usability. In a data warehousing context, data stewards are responsible for maintaining consistent definitions, resolving data conflicts, ensuring data integrity, and supporting data governance policies. They work closely with IT and business teams to monitor data throughout its lifecycle. Data stewardship helps in enforcing data standards, building trust in analytics, and enhancing the reliability of the data warehouse for decision-making.

106. What is hybrid data warehousing?
Answer: Hybrid data warehousing combines on-premise and cloud-based data storage and processing architectures. It allows organizations to maintain critical data securely in-house while leveraging the scalability and flexibility of the cloud for analytics and reporting. This approach supports various workloads, reduces infrastructure costs, and facilitates modernization without complete migration. Hybrid models often integrate legacy systems with cloud-native platforms using tools like data virtualization, APIs, and cloud connectors. They are ideal for organizations transitioning to cloud while maintaining regulatory or operational requirements for on-premise data.

107. What is the role of cloud computing in modern data warehousing?
Answer: Cloud computing has revolutionized data warehousing by offering scalable, cost-effective, and flexible solutions. Cloud-based data warehouses like Amazon Redshift, Google BigQuery, and Snowflake eliminate the need for heavy infrastructure and provide on-demand resources. They support real-time analytics, automatic scaling, and high availability. Cloud platforms also integrate with big data tools, machine learning services, and data lakes. This empowers organizations to store, process, and analyze massive datasets efficiently. Cloud computing facilitates quicker deployments, improved collaboration, and global accessibility, making it a key component of modern data warehousing.

108. What is schema evolution in data warehouses?
Answer: Schema evolution refers to the ability of a data warehouse to adapt to changes in its structure without losing existing data or disrupting operations. These changes may include adding or deleting columns, changing data types, or updating relationships. Schema evolution is crucial in dynamic business environments where data sources, formats, and reporting needs frequently change. Data warehouses must support versioning, backward compatibility, and metadata updates to manage schema evolution effectively. Failure to do so can result in data inconsistency and analytical errors.

109. What is temporal data in data warehousing?
Answer: Temporal data refers to data that changes over time and includes time-related aspects such as historical, current, and future states. In data warehousing, temporal data allows analysts to perform time-based queries, compare trends, and maintain history through slowly changing dimensions (SCDs). It is critical for tracking performance over periods, forecasting, and compliance reporting. Temporal modeling includes valid time (real-world time) and transaction time (database time). Managing temporal data involves capturing change history and ensuring time-based consistency for accurate decision-making.

110. What is a materialized view in a data warehouse?
Answer: A materialized view is a precomputed table that stores the result of a query, such as aggregations or joins, to improve query performance in a data warehouse. Unlike regular views, materialized views are physically stored and can be refreshed periodically or on-demand. They reduce query time by avoiding repetitive computation and are useful in OLAP and reporting systems. Materialized views are particularly beneficial in large-scale data warehouses where complex queries on vast datasets are common. They also support summary management and optimization techniques.

111. What is the difference between ETL and ELT in data processing?
Answer: ETL (Extract, Transform, Load) involves extracting data from source systems, transforming it to fit analytical requirements, and then loading it into the data warehouse. ELT (Extract, Load, Transform) first loads raw data into the target system and performs transformations within the warehouse, often using its processing power. ETL is suitable

for traditional on-premise systems, while ELT is optimized for modern cloud-based warehouses that support in-database processing. The choice depends on data volume, architecture, and performance requirements.

112. What is OLAP cube browsing?
Answer: OLAP cube browsing refers to navigating and analyzing multidimensional data stored in OLAP cubes. Users can explore dimensions such as time, geography, and product categories by drilling down, slicing, dicing, and pivoting the data. This enables flexible and fast ad-hoc analysis. OLAP browsing tools often include interactive dashboards and visualizations. It empowers users to derive insights, compare metrics, and identify patterns without needing deep technical skills. Efficient cube browsing supports decision-makers with immediate access to summarized and detailed data.

113. What is columnar storage in data warehousing?
Answer: Columnar storage is a data storage format in which data is stored column-wise rather than row-wise. It is particularly effective in data warehousing environments that involve analytical queries on large datasets. Columnar databases read only relevant columns, reducing I/O and improving performance for aggregation and filtering tasks. This format also allows better compression, faster data scans, and more efficient use of memory. Examples of columnar databases include Amazon Redshift, Apache Parquet, and Google BigQuery. Columnar storage is ideal for OLAP and big data analytics.

114. What is star schema optimization?
Answer: Star schema optimization involves techniques to enhance the performance and usability of star schemas in data warehousing. Optimization may include indexing fact and dimension tables, denormalizing dimension tables to reduce joins, and creating aggregate tables or materialized views. Partitioning large fact tables and using surrogate keys also improve efficiency. Star schema optimization ensures fast response times for analytical queries and supports complex business intelligence operations. Proper design and tuning are essential to ensure scalability and usability in high-volume environments.

115. What is data vault modeling?
Answer: Data vault modeling is a data warehousing methodology designed to handle large-scale, rapidly changing data environments. It separates data into three components: hubs (business keys), links (relationships), and satellites (descriptive data). This structure allows for scalability, auditability, and historical tracking while supporting agile development. Data vaults are highly normalized and support parallel loading, making them suitable for modern data integration tasks. Compared to traditional star or snowflake models, data vaults offer better adaptability and long-term maintainability.

116. What is a dashboard in data warehousing?
Answer: A dashboard is a visual interface that displays key performance indicators (KPIs), metrics, and analytics derived from a data warehouse. Dashboards provide real-time or periodic summaries of business performance using charts, graphs, and tables. They help users monitor trends, identify anomalies, and make informed decisions. Dashboards are tailored to specific roles (e.g., finance, sales) and are often interactive, allowing filtering, drill-down, and export. Effective dashboards enhance transparency, accountability, and strategic planning by making complex data understandable at a glance.

117. What is a KPI in the context of data analytics?
Answer: A Key Performance Indicator (KPI) is a quantifiable metric used to evaluate the success of an organization or a specific activity. In the context of data warehousing and analytics, KPIs are derived from data stored in the warehouse and are used in reports and dashboards. Examples include sales growth, customer churn rate, and inventory turnover. KPIs align business objectives with measurable outcomes and help stakeholders monitor progress and take corrective actions. Well-defined KPIs are specific, measurable, and actionable, forming the foundation of data-driven decision-making.

118. What is the difference between structured and unstructured data in warehousing?
Answer: Structured data refers to data that follows a predefined format, such as rows and columns in relational databases. It is easily searchable and manageable using SQL. Unstructured data lacks a fixed schema and includes formats like text, images, videos, and emails. While traditional data warehouses are designed for structured data, modern systems incorporate data lakes and hybrid models to handle unstructured data. Tools like Hadoop and NoSQL

databases help store and process unstructured content. Understanding both types is essential for comprehensive analytics and business insights.

119. What is the role of data cleansing in data warehousing?
Answer: Data cleansing is the process of identifying and correcting errors, inconsistencies, and inaccuracies in data before loading it into a data warehouse. It includes tasks like removing duplicates, standardizing formats, correcting typos, and filling missing values. Clean data ensures accuracy in analysis and builds trust in business intelligence outputs. Data cleansing is typically part of the ETL process and may be automated using tools like OpenRefine, Talend, or Python scripts. High-quality data is essential for making informed, confident decisions and maintaining system reliability.

120. What is a data catalog?
Answer: A data catalog is an organized inventory of data assets within an organization, including metadata, data lineage, and business glossary. In data warehousing, it helps users discover, understand, and manage available data. Data catalogs improve data governance, compliance, and self-service analytics. They often include search functionality, access controls, and collaboration features. By promoting data literacy and transparency, data catalogs make it easier for analysts and stakeholders to access the right data for analysis and decision-making.

121. What is a data mart and how does it differ from a data warehouse?
Answer: A data mart is a subset of a data warehouse focused on a specific business function, such as sales, finance, or marketing. It is designed to meet the needs of a particular department or user group. Data marts are smaller, faster to implement, and can operate independently or as part of a larger warehouse ecosystem. In contrast, a data warehouse is a centralized repository for the entire organization's data. While data warehouses support enterprise-wide analysis, data marts offer targeted insights and simplify access for specialized users.

122. What is the concept of drill-down analysis?
Answer: Drill-down analysis is a technique used in OLAP and dashboards that allows users to move from summarized data to more detailed levels. For example, a sales report might start with total sales by year and let users drill down to sales by quarter, month, or region. This interactive feature helps uncover underlying trends, identify root causes, and perform deeper analysis without running new queries. Drill-down enhances the usability of data warehouses by providing intuitive exploration and decision support.

123. What is data auditing in a warehouse?
Answer: Data auditing involves tracking, validating, and ensuring the accuracy and integrity of data as it flows through the data warehouse. It includes monitoring ETL processes, verifying record counts, logging changes, and detecting anomalies. Auditing helps identify data quality issues, unauthorized changes, or system failures. It supports compliance with regulatory requirements such as GDPR and SOX. Implementing effective data auditing mechanisms improves transparency, accountability, and confidence in data-driven processes.

124. What is a query performance bottleneck and how can it be resolved?
Answer: A query performance bottleneck occurs when data retrieval is slow due to inefficient queries, poor indexing, or hardware limitations. In data warehousing, this impacts user experience and decision-making. Solutions include query optimization, indexing, partitioning large tables, and caching frequently accessed results. Using materialized views, tuning the database engine, and distributing the workload can also help. Regular monitoring and database profiling tools are essential to diagnose and resolve bottlenecks efficiently.

125. What is a dimensional data model?
Answer: A dimensional data model is a design approach used in data warehousing that organizes data into fact and dimension tables. Fact tables contain quantitative data (measurable metrics), while dimension tables hold descriptive attributes (e.g., time, location, product). This model supports fast, flexible querying and reporting through schemas like star and snowflake. It aligns closely with business processes and enhances user understanding of data. Dimensional modeling is essential for building effective OLAP systems and is foundational in most business intelligence solutions.

126. What is surrogate key in data warehousing?
Answer: A surrogate key is an artificial or system-generated key used in data warehousing to uniquely identify records

in a dimension table. Unlike natural keys (which are derived from business data), surrogate keys have no inherent meaning and are usually integers assigned by the system. They help maintain consistency and track changes in slowly changing dimensions (SCDs). Surrogate keys simplify joins between fact and dimension tables and protect against changes in natural keys. They are widely used in star and snowflake schemas to ensure integrity and simplify ETL processes.

127. What is metadata repository in a data warehouse?
Answer: A metadata repository is a centralized database that stores metadata—data about the data—in a data warehouse. It includes technical metadata (such as data types, sources, and lineage), business metadata (definitions, rules, and calculations), and operational metadata (load schedules, error logs). The repository helps users understand data origin, meaning, and usage. It also supports ETL management, data governance, and troubleshooting. A well-maintained metadata repository enhances transparency, data discovery, and the efficiency of data warehousing operations.

128. What is partitioning and why is it important in data warehouses?
Answer: Partitioning is the process of dividing large database tables into smaller, manageable segments or partitions based on certain criteria, such as range, list, or hash values. In data warehouses, partitioning improves query performance, simplifies data maintenance, and optimizes data loading. For instance, time-based partitioning allows faster access to recent data while archiving older data efficiently. Partitioning also helps in parallel processing, which boosts scalability and reduces response time for large analytical queries. It is a key optimization technique in high-volume data environments.

129. What are data warehouse appliances?
Answer: Data warehouse appliances are pre-configured hardware and software systems designed specifically for data warehousing and analytical processing. They combine compute, storage, database, and ETL components into a single integrated solution. Examples include Oracle Exadata, IBM Netezza, and Teradata. These appliances are optimized for high-performance analytics, support massive parallel processing (MPP), and offer rapid deployment. They simplify infrastructure management and reduce the complexity of building and maintaining a traditional data warehouse architecture.

130. What is cube aggregation in OLAP systems?
Answer: Cube aggregation refers to the process of summarizing data along one or more dimensions in an OLAP cube. It involves calculating aggregate measures such as totals, averages, or counts across various hierarchies (e.g., monthly sales rolled up to quarterly or yearly sales). Aggregation reduces query time and enables fast access to summarized insights. Pre-aggregated cubes are especially useful in large data sets where on-the-fly computation would be resource-intensive. This functionality is essential for efficient multidimensional analysis in data warehouses.

9 789369 725

Printed at Repro India Ltd.